Learning Bengali Alphabet

for English speakers

by Isaul Karim

This book is dedicated to my children
Eiliyah, Raihan and Ibaadah

Copyright © Isaul Karim 2017
All rights reserved. No part of this publication
may be reproduced, stored in a retrieval system, or transmitted,
in any form or by any means, electronics, mechanical,
photocopying, recording or otherwise,
without the permission
of the author.

Bengali Alphabet

As well as having vowels and consonants, Bengali alphabet also has vowel marks and modifiers. All will be explained in this book, one by one. First, we will look at the vowels which are given below. In the next few pages we will learn the name of each vowel, the sound they make, and how to write each letter.

vowels

অ   আ   ই   ঈ   উ   ঊ

ঋ   এ   ঐ   ও   ঔ

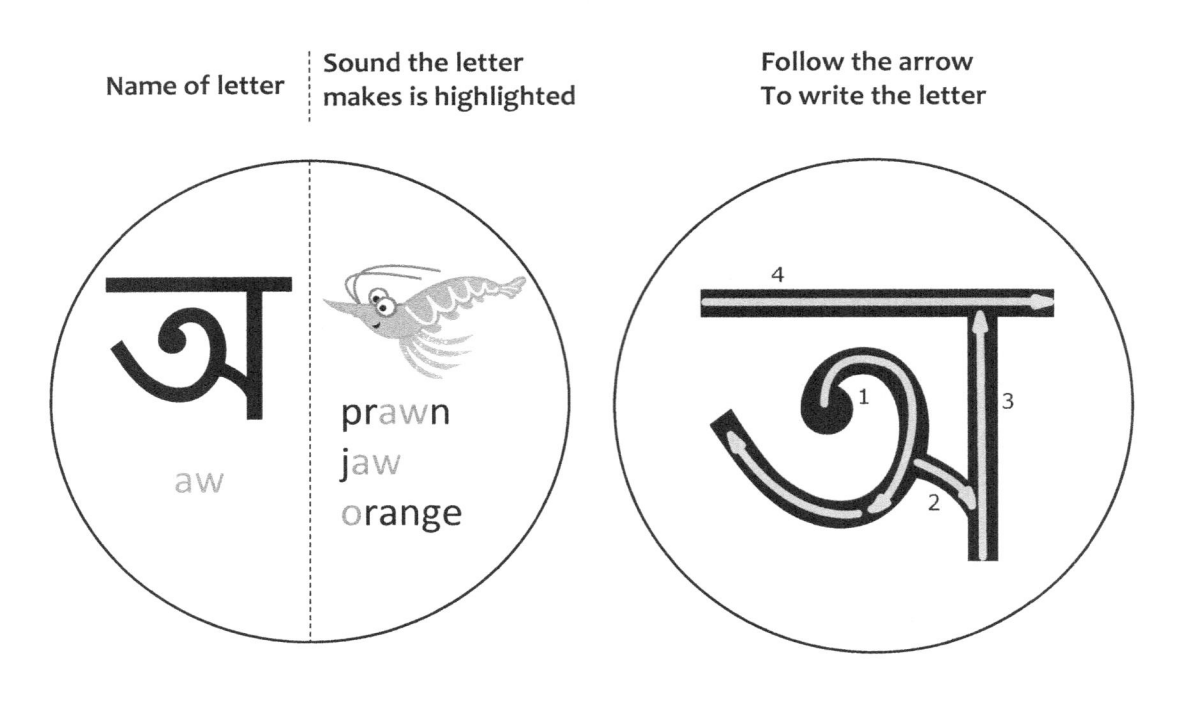

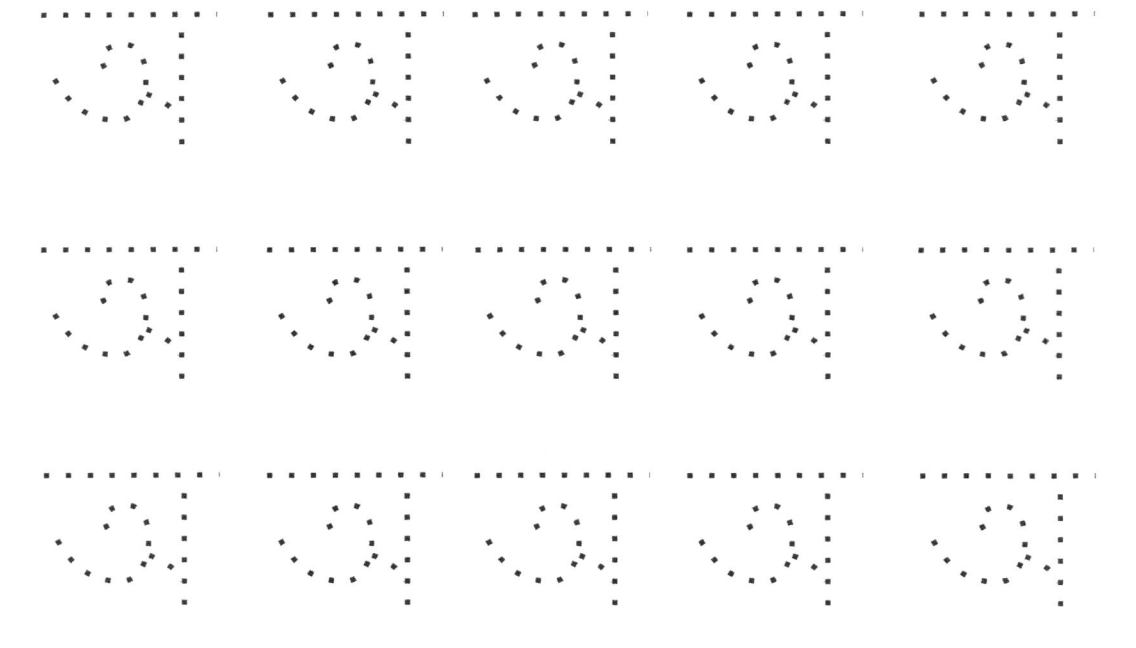

Name of letter | Sound the letter makes is highlighted

Follow the arrow
To write the letter

অ

aw

pr**aw**n
j**aw**
orange

2

| Name of letter | Sound the letter makes is highlighted | Follow the arrow To write the letter |

আ

ah

bunny
done
come

3

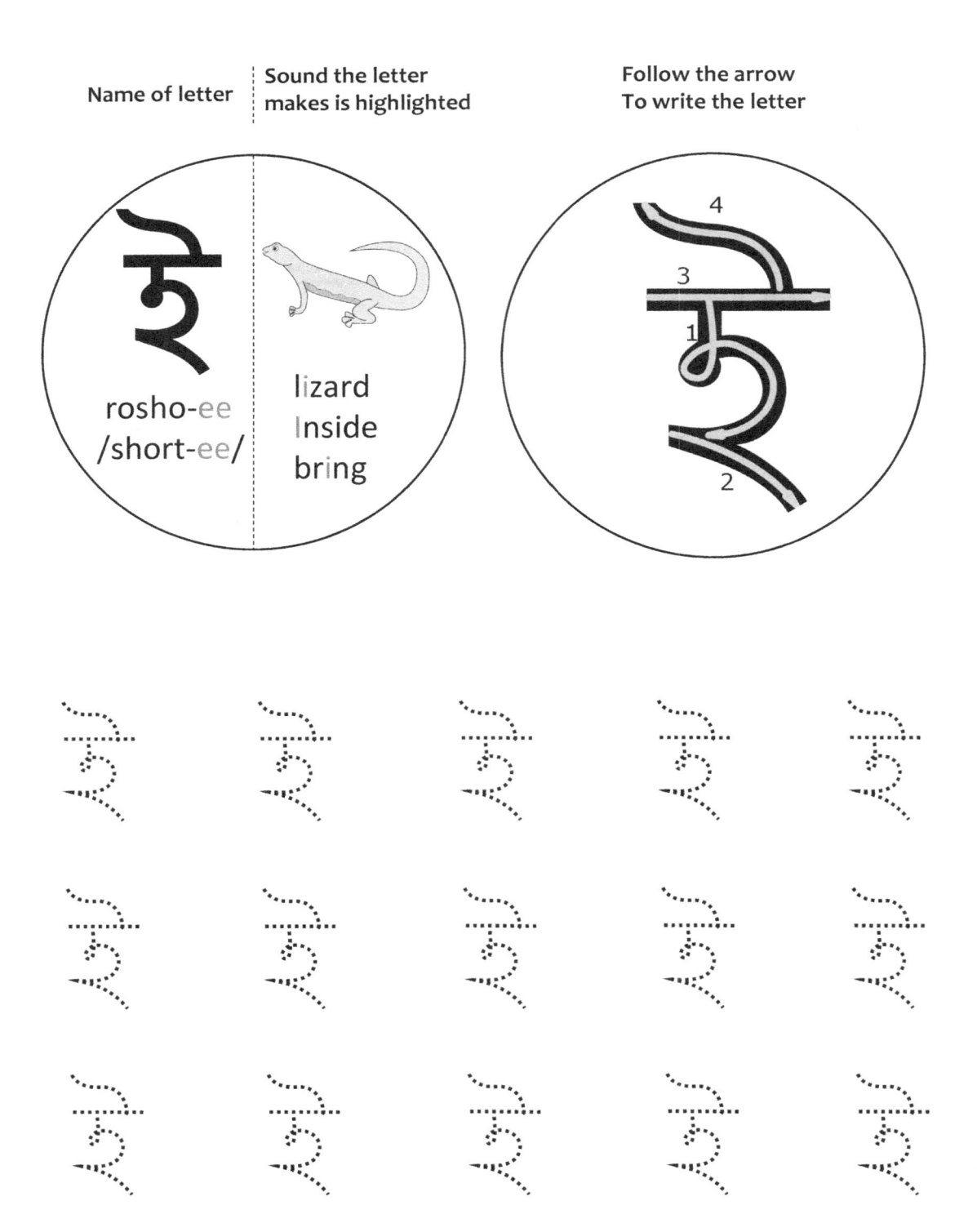

Name of letter	Sound the letter makes is highlighted	Follow the arrow To write the letter
ই rosho-ee /short-ee/	lizard Inside bring	

| Name of letter | Sound the letter makes is highlighted | Follow the arrow To write the letter |

ঈ

dirgo-ee
/long-ee/

eagle
feat
feast

5

| Name of letter | Sound the letter makes is highlighted | Follow the arrow To write the letter |

উ

rosho-oo /short-oo/

s**oo**p b**oo**k l**oo**k

Name of letter | Sound the letter makes is highlighted

Follow the arrow
To write the letter

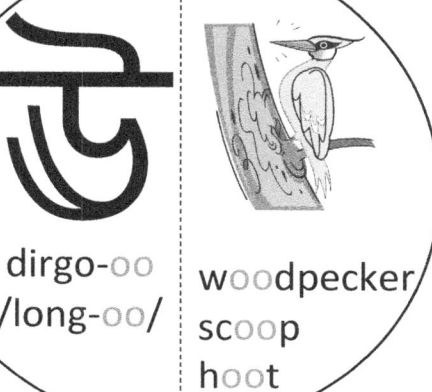

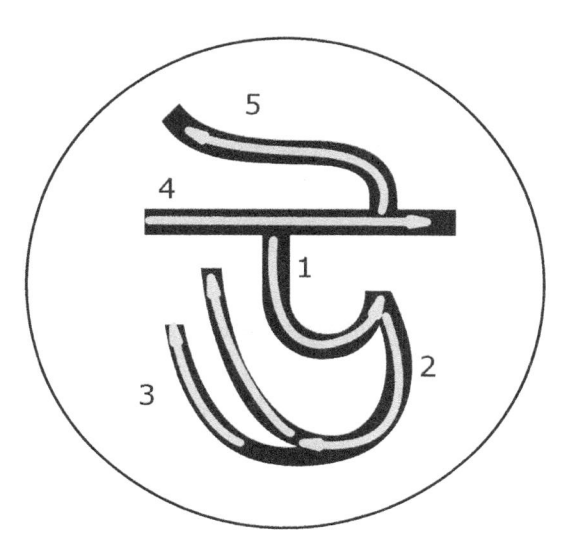

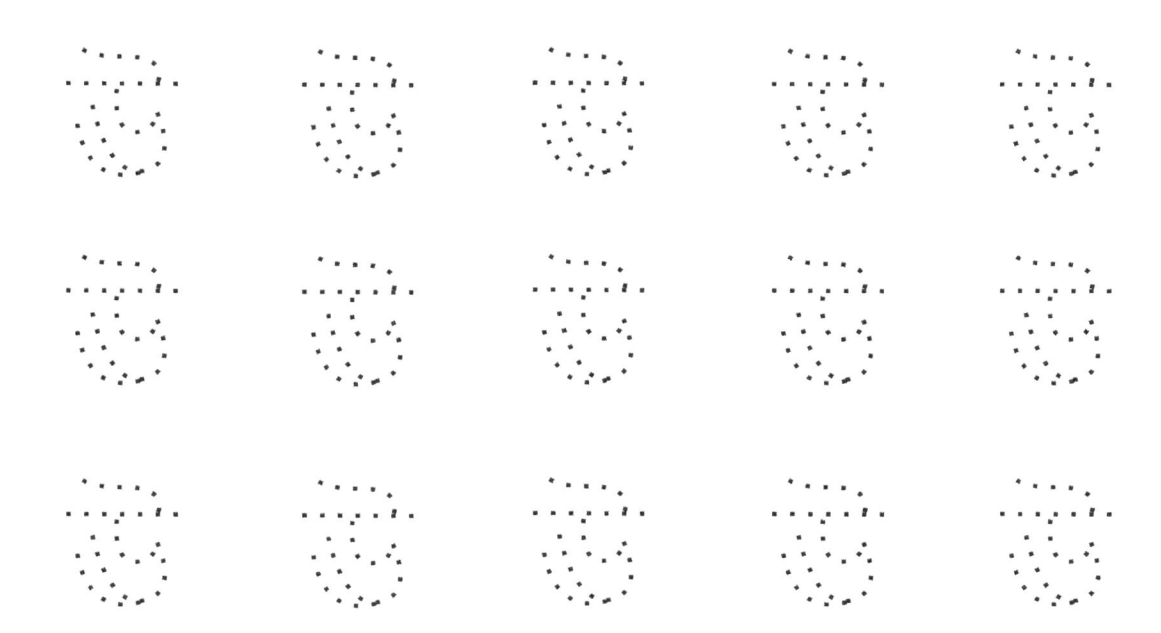

dirgo-oo
/long-oo/

woodpecker
scoop
hoot

7

Draw a line to connect each letter to it's name

অ	ah
আ	aw
ই	dirgo-ee /long-ee/
ঈ	rosho-oo /short-oo/
উ	rosho-ee /short-ee/
ঊ	dirgo-oo /long-oo/

Name of letter | Sound the letter makes is highlighted

Follow the arrow
To write the letter

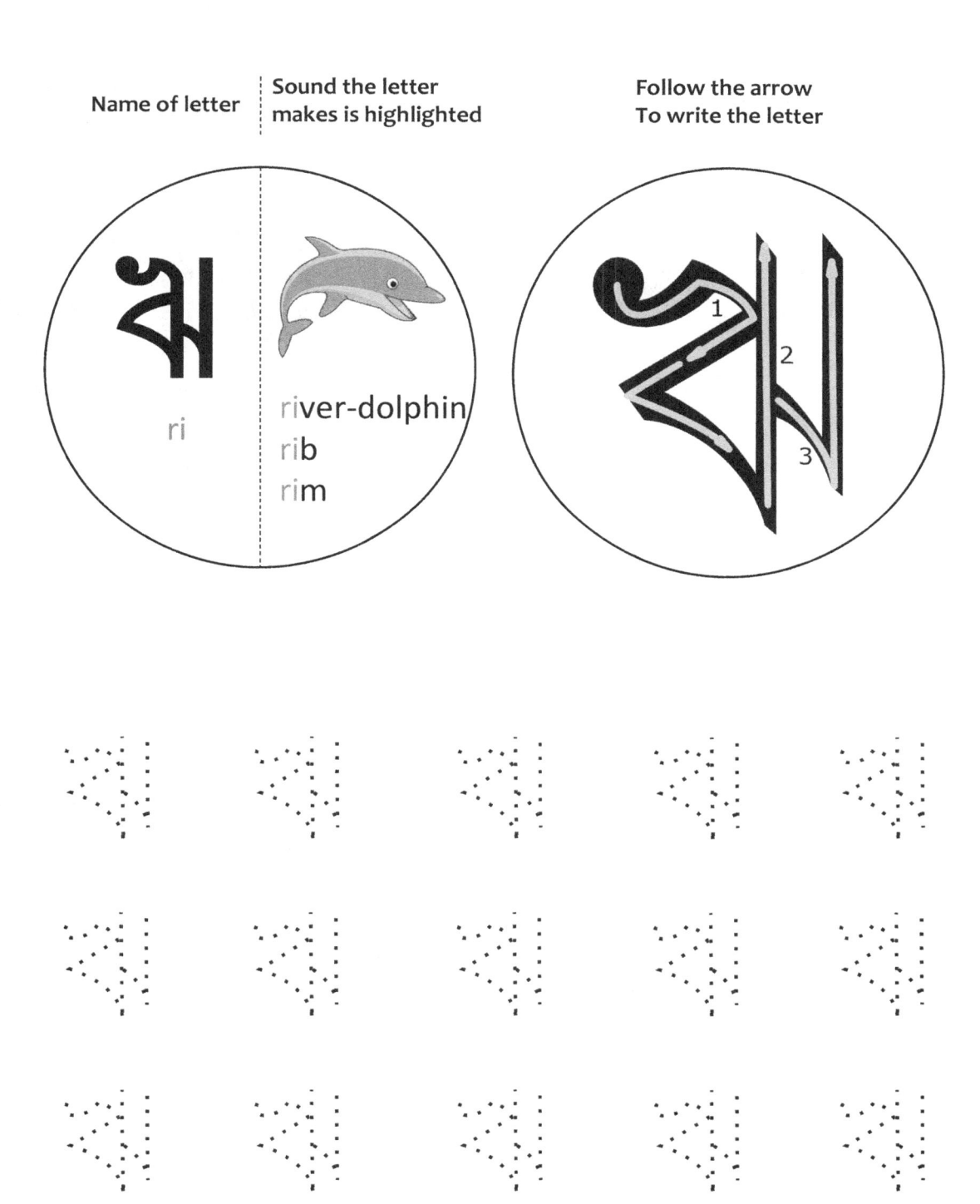

ঋ

ri

river-dolphin
rib
rim

Name of letter | Sound the letter makes is highlighted

Follow the arrow
To write the letter

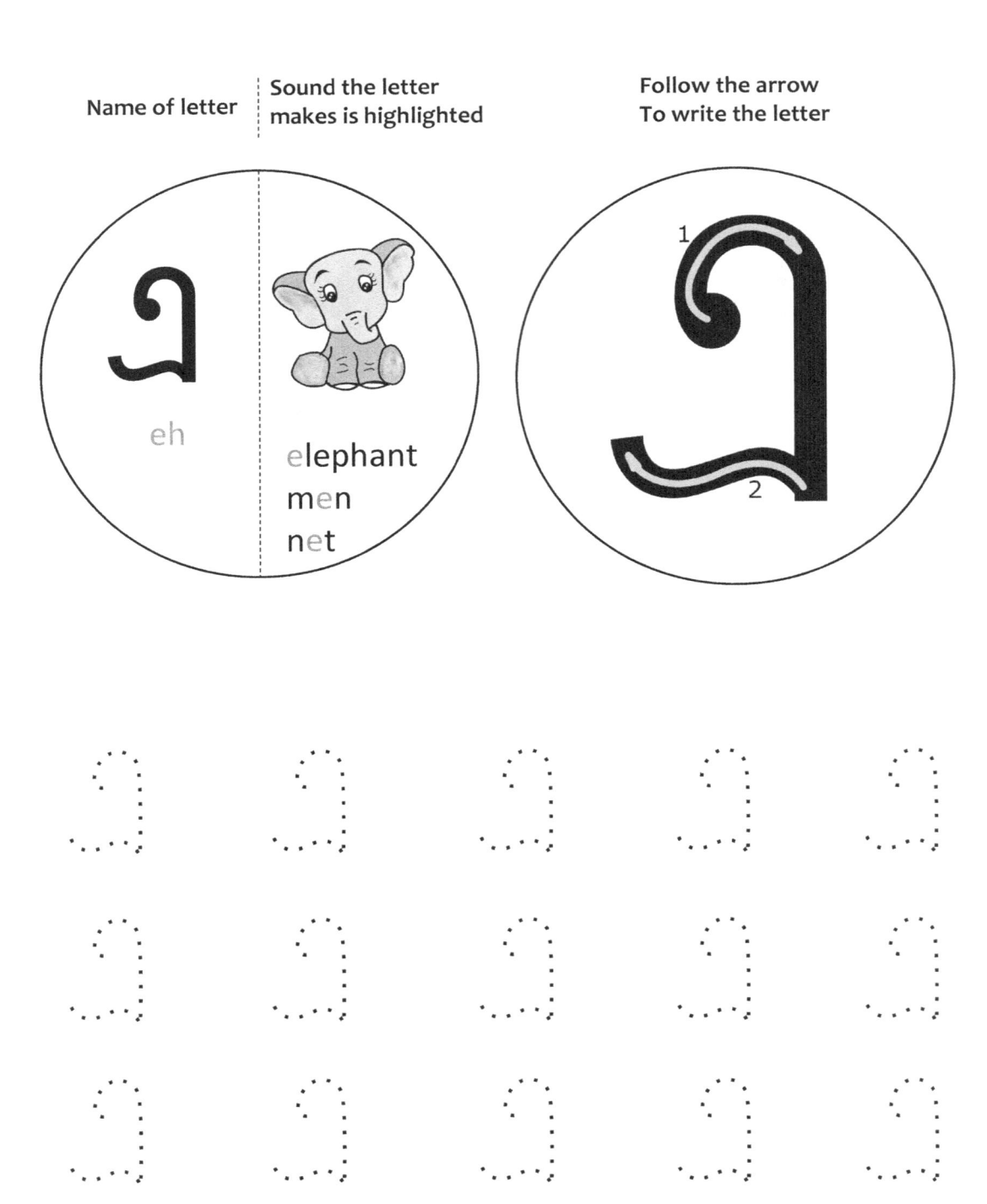

eh

elephant
m e n
n e t

Name of letter | Sound the letter makes is highlighted

Follow the arrow
To write the letter

ঐ

oi

oyster
l**oy**al
r**oy**al

11

Name of letter | Sound the letter makes is highlighted

Follow the arrow
To write the letter

au

sauce
launch
haunt

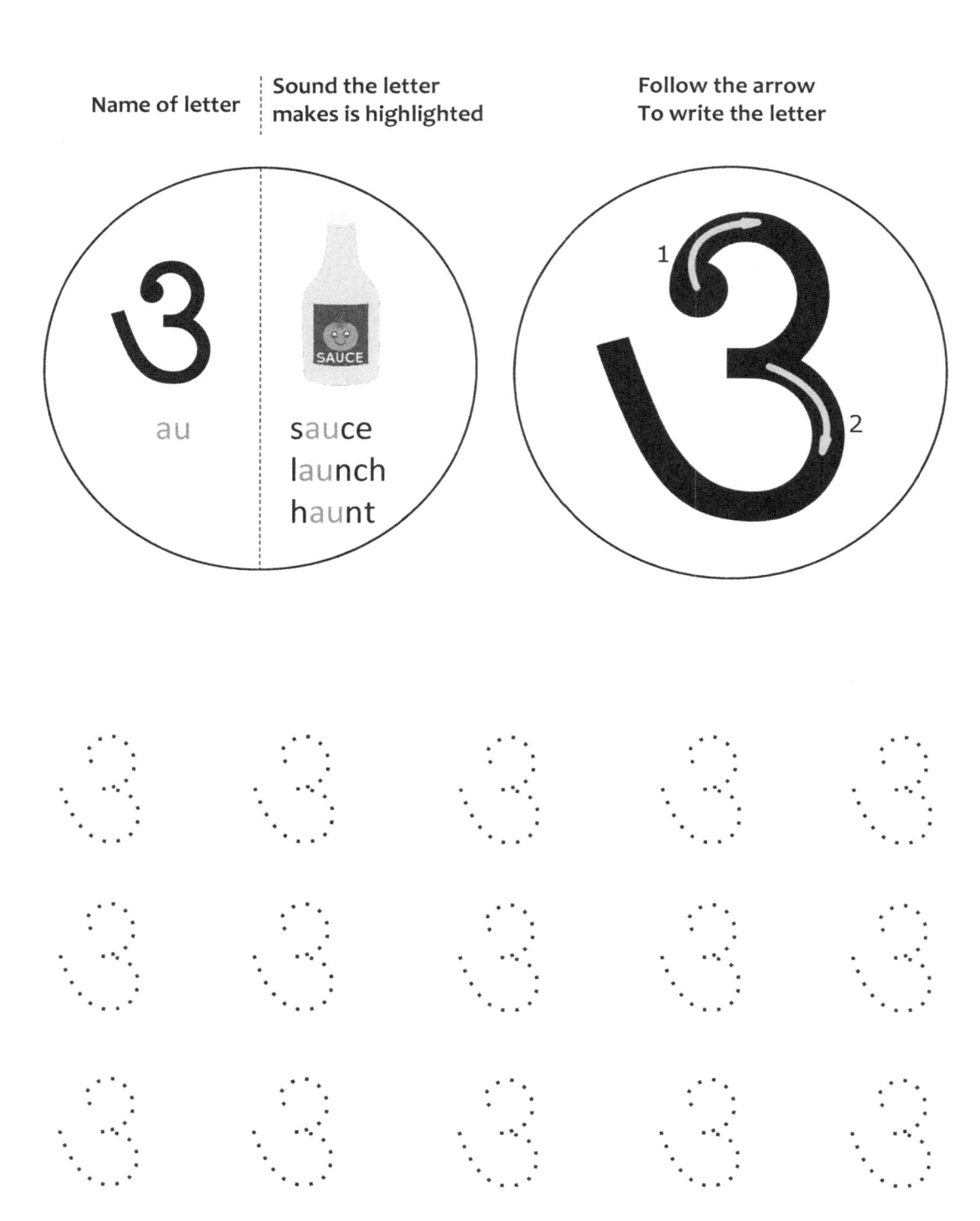

12

Name of letter | **Sound the letter makes is highlighted** | **Follow the arrow To write the letter**

ow

cr**ow**
b**ow**
g**o**

13

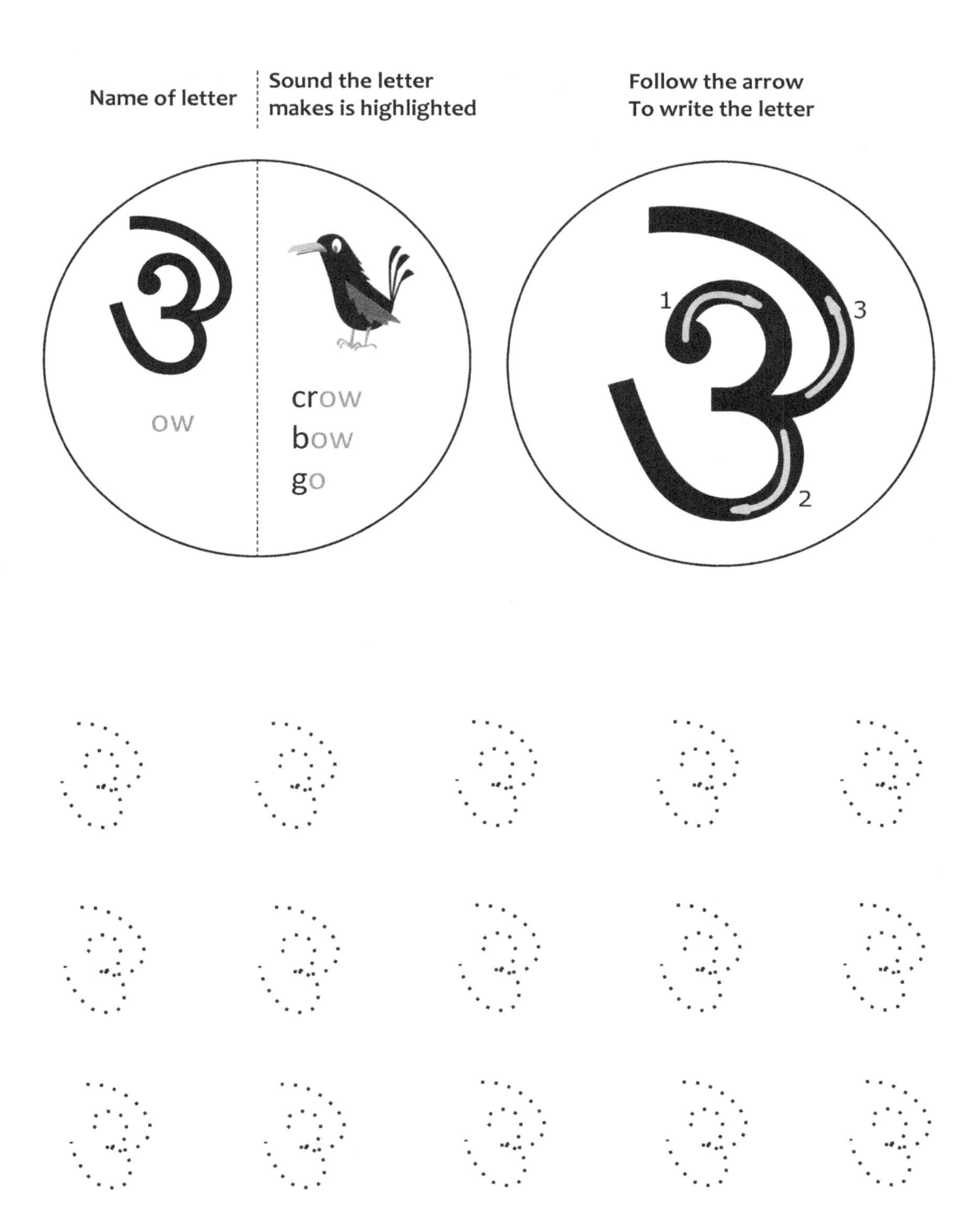

Draw a line to connect each letter to it's name

ঋ	eh
এ	au
ঌ	ri
ও	ow
ঔ	oi

Consonants

ক	খ	গ	ঘ	ঙ
চ	ছ	জ	ঝ	ঞ
ট	ঠ	ড	ঢ	ণ
ত	থ	দ	ধ	ন
প	ফ	ব	ভ	ম
য	র	ল	শ	ষ
স	হ	ড়	ঢ়	য়
ৎ	্ঃ			

| Name of letter | Sound the letter makes is highlighted | Follow the arrow To write the letter |

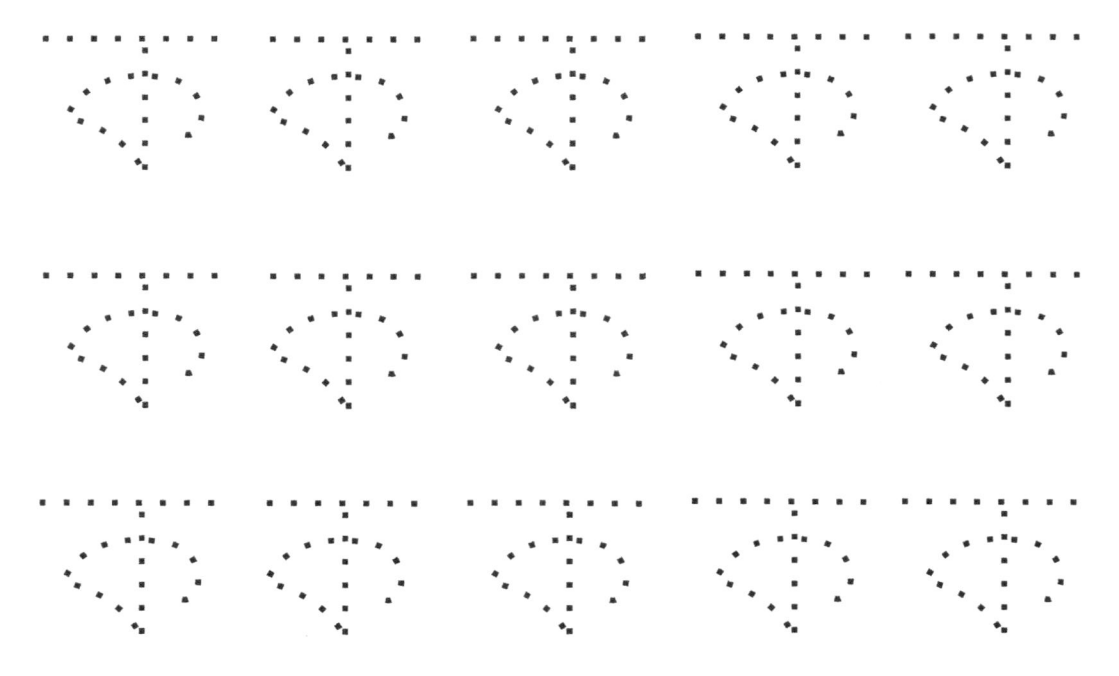

ক

kaw

cot
cat
kind

Name of letter	Sound the letter makes is highlighted	Follow the arrow To write the letter

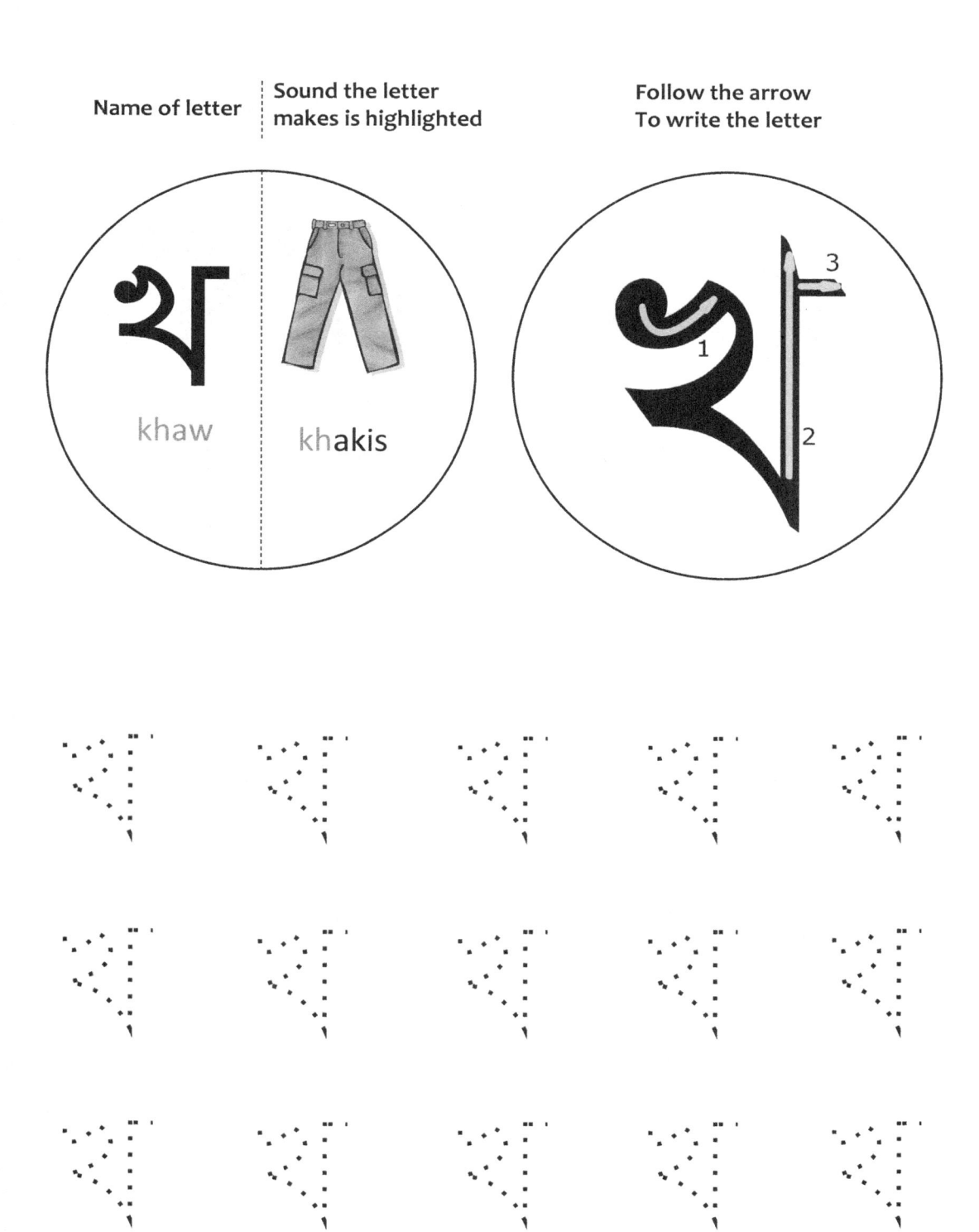

khaw | khakis

17

| Name of letter | Sound the letter makes is highlighted | Follow the arrow To write the letter |

গ

gaw

gorilla
goat
gone

18

Name of letter	Sound the letter makes is highlighted	Follow the arrow To write the letter

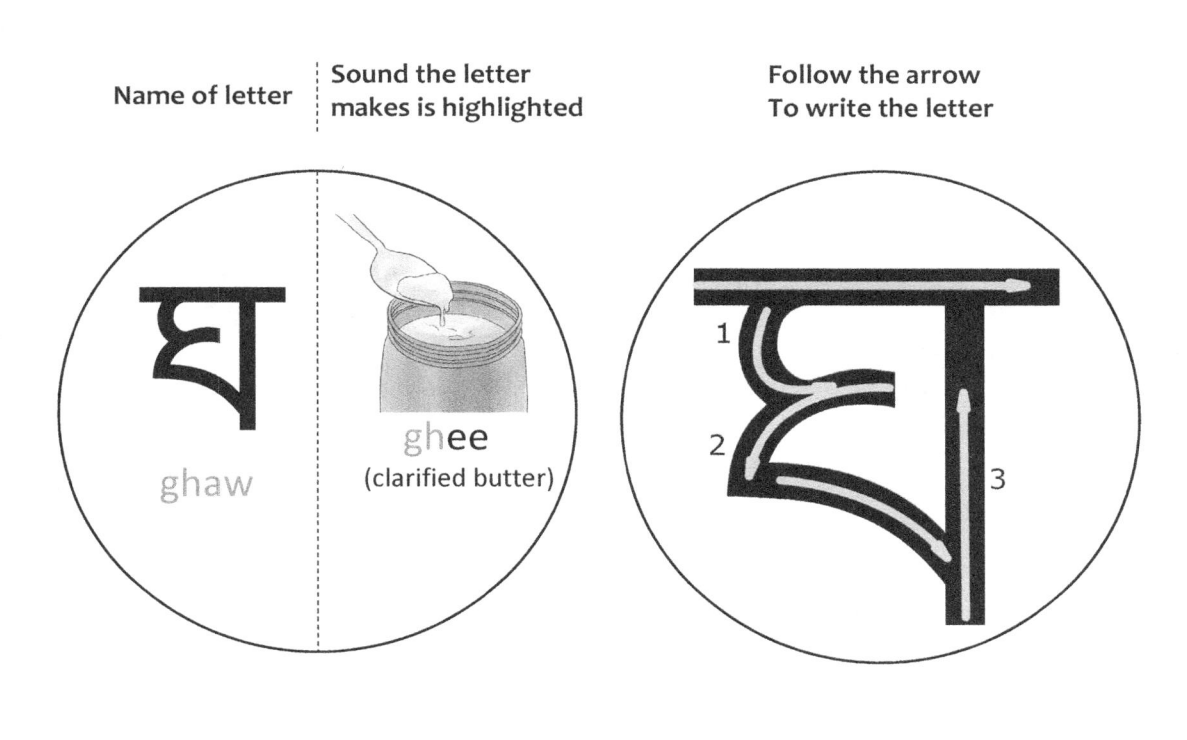

ঘ
ghaw

ghee
(clarified butter)

19

Name of letter | Sound the letter makes is highlighted

Follow the arrow
To write the letter

ungo

ba**ng**
sti**ng**
si**ng**

20

Draw a line to connect each letter to it's name

ক	gaw
খ	khaw
গ	ungo
ঘ	kaw
ঙ	ghaw

| Name of letter | Sound the letter makes is highlighted | Follow the arrow To write the letter |

chaw

watch
hatch
latch

Name of letter	Sound the letter makes is highlighted	Follow the arrow To write the letter
ছ chhaw	chick child chill	

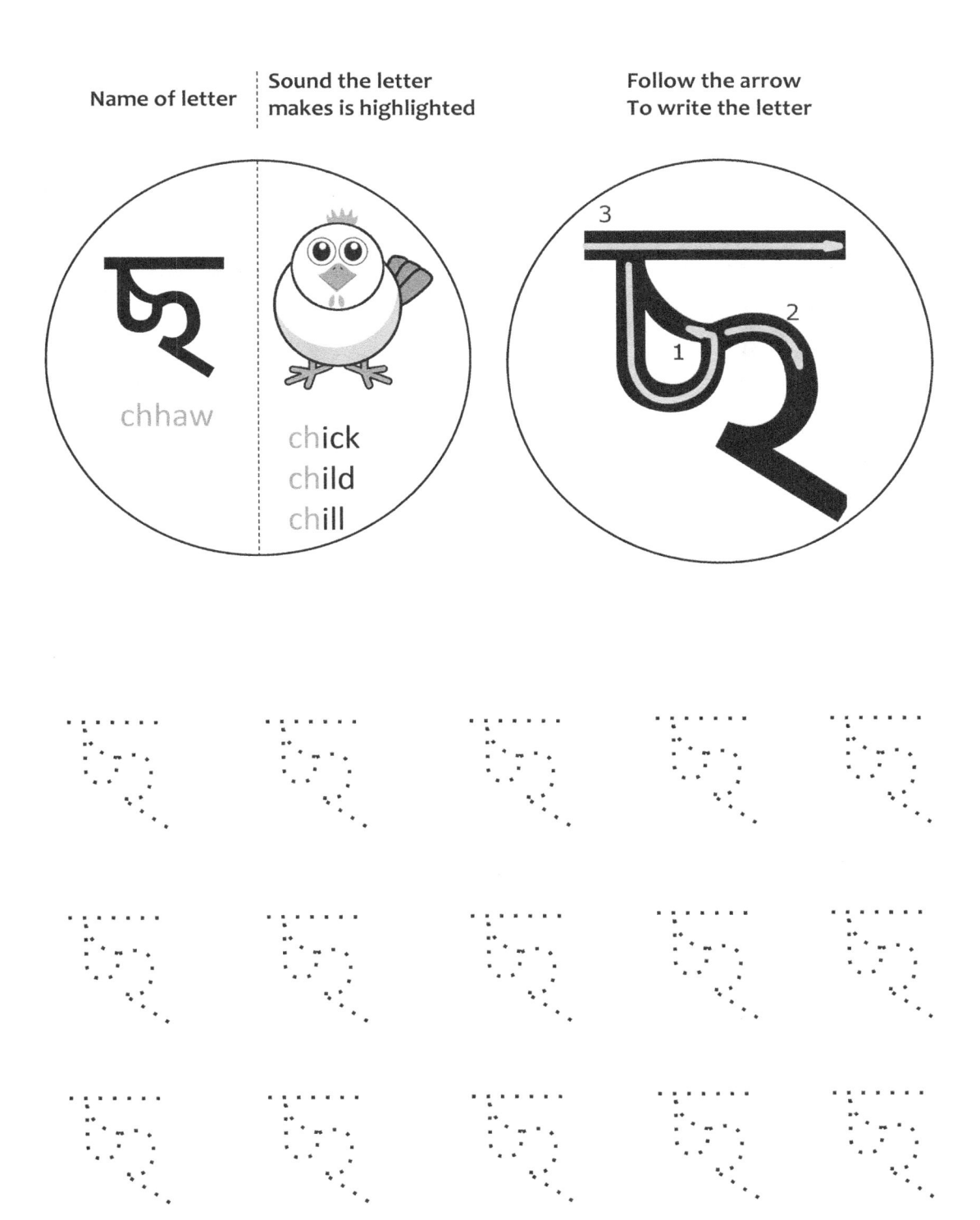

23

Name of letter | Sound the letter makes is highlighted

Follow the arrow
To write the letter

borgiyo-jaw

giraffe
age
cage

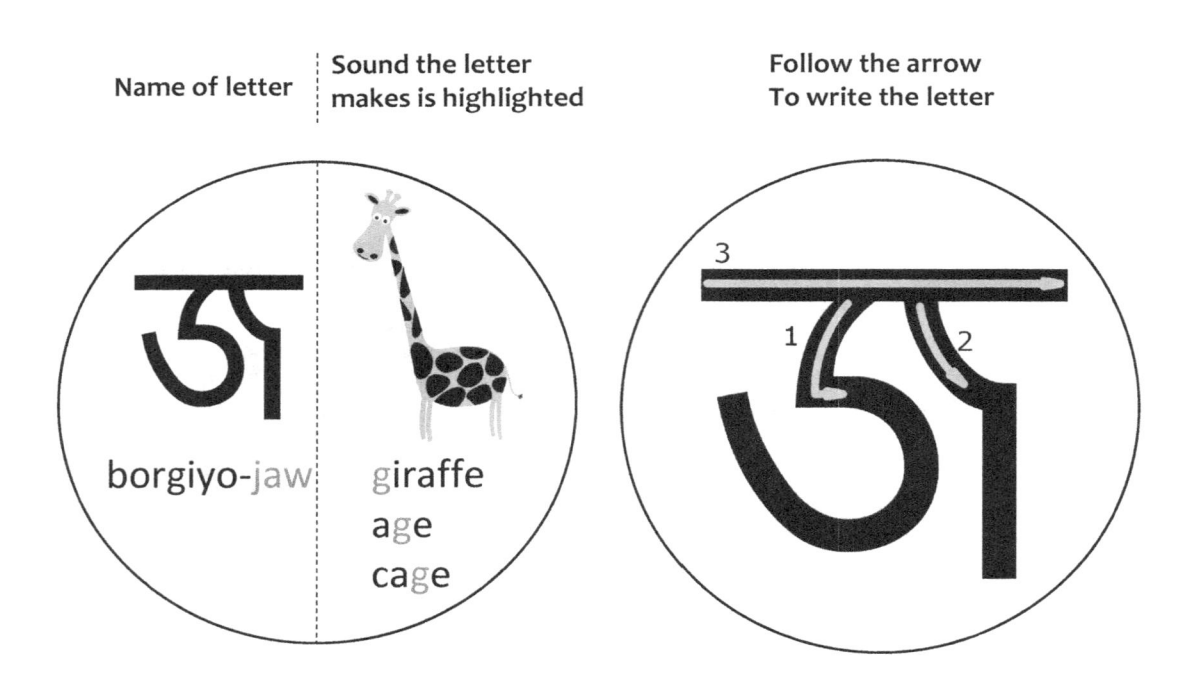

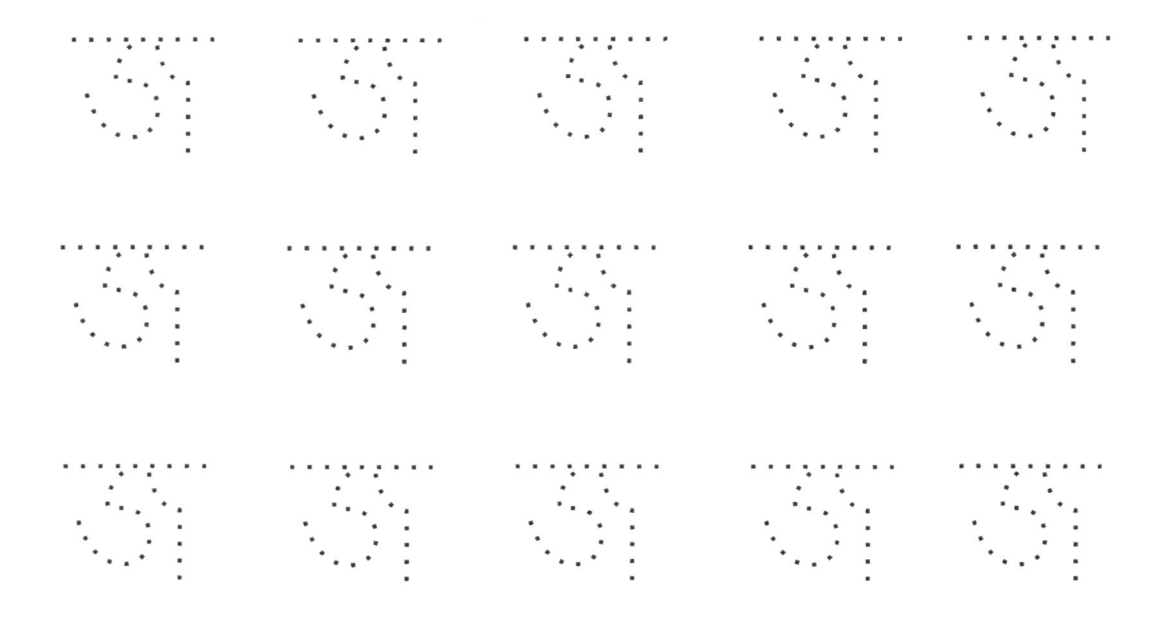

24

Name of letter	Sound the letter makes is highlighted	Follow the arrow To write the letter

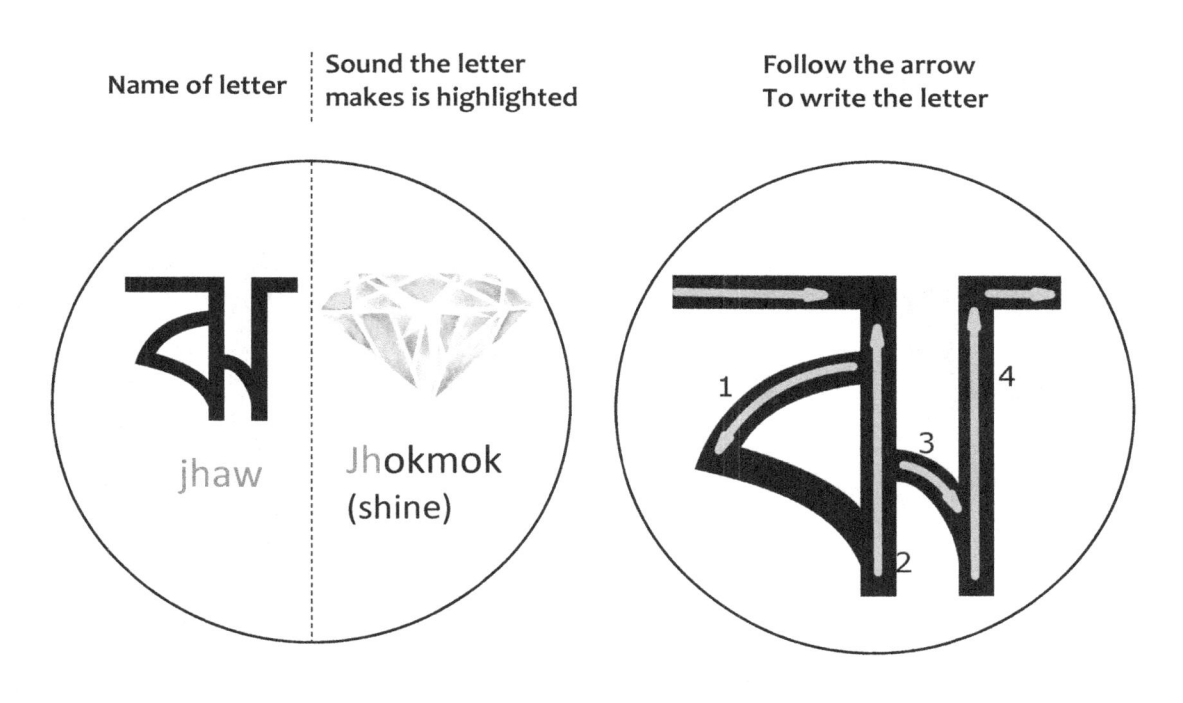

ঝ jhaw — Jhokmok (shine)

| Name of letter | Sound the letter makes is highlighted | Follow the arrow To write the letter |

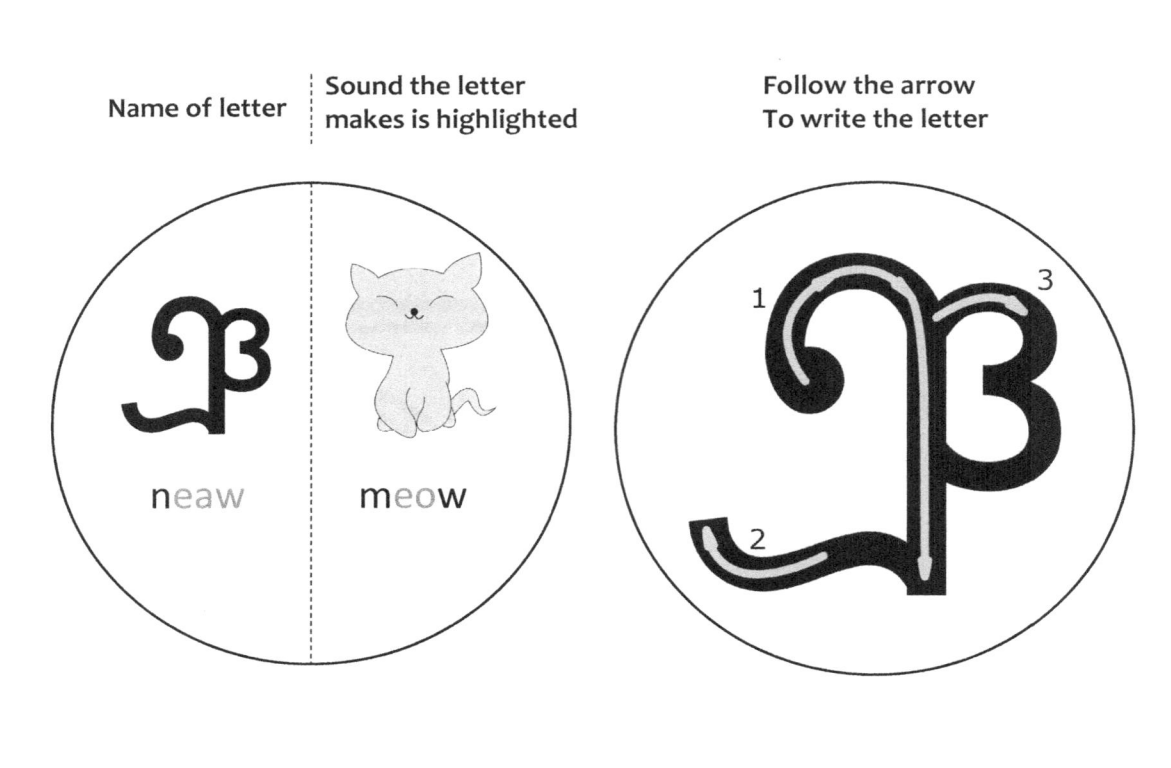

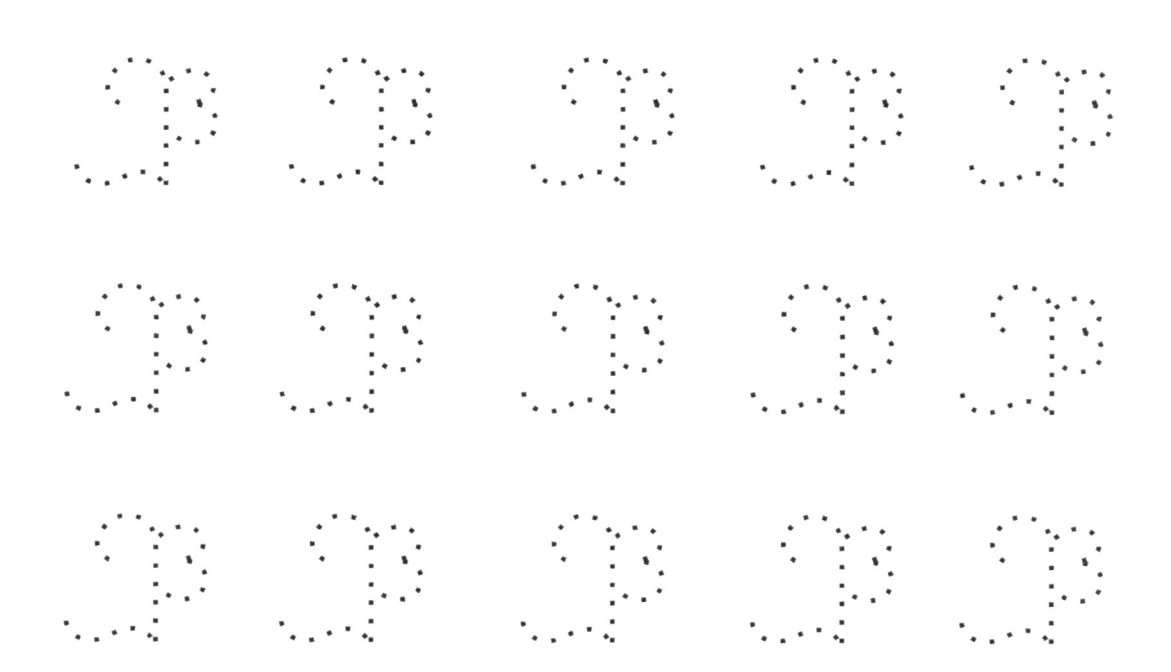

n**eaw** | m**eo**w

26

Draw a line to connect each letter to it's name

চ	jhaw
ছ	chaw
জ	chhaw
ঝ	neaw
ঞ	borgiyo-jaw

| Name of letter | Sound the letter makes is highlighted | Follow the arrow To write the letter |

ট

taw

turtle
tin
tango

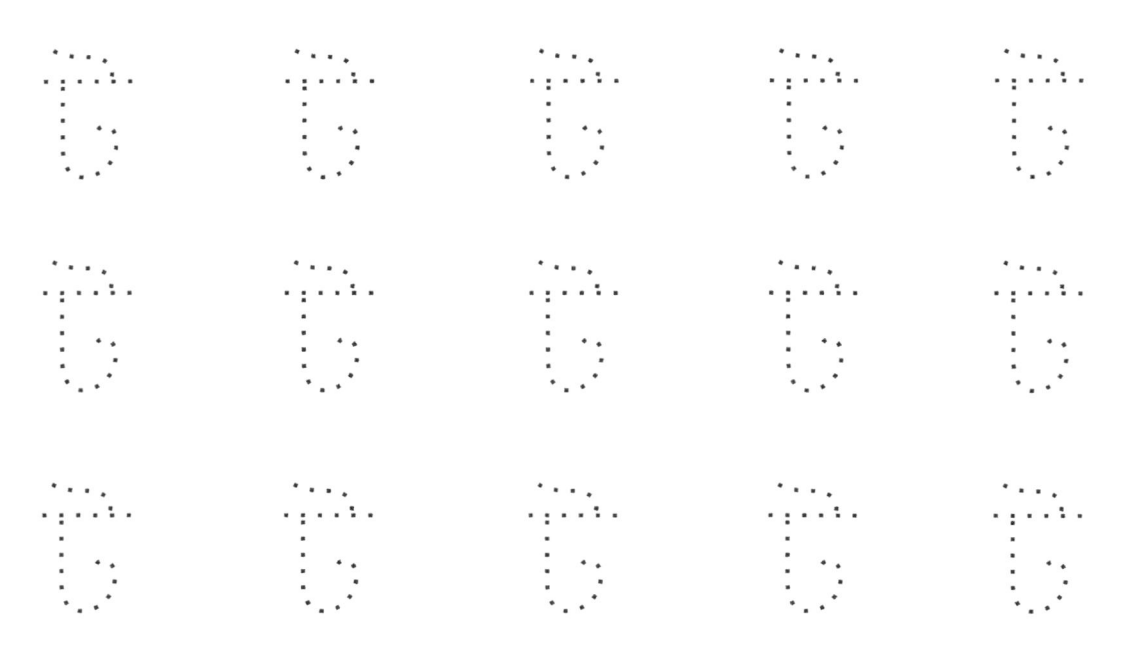

| Name of letter | Sound the letter makes is highlighted | Follow the arrow To write the letter |

ttaw o**tt**er

29

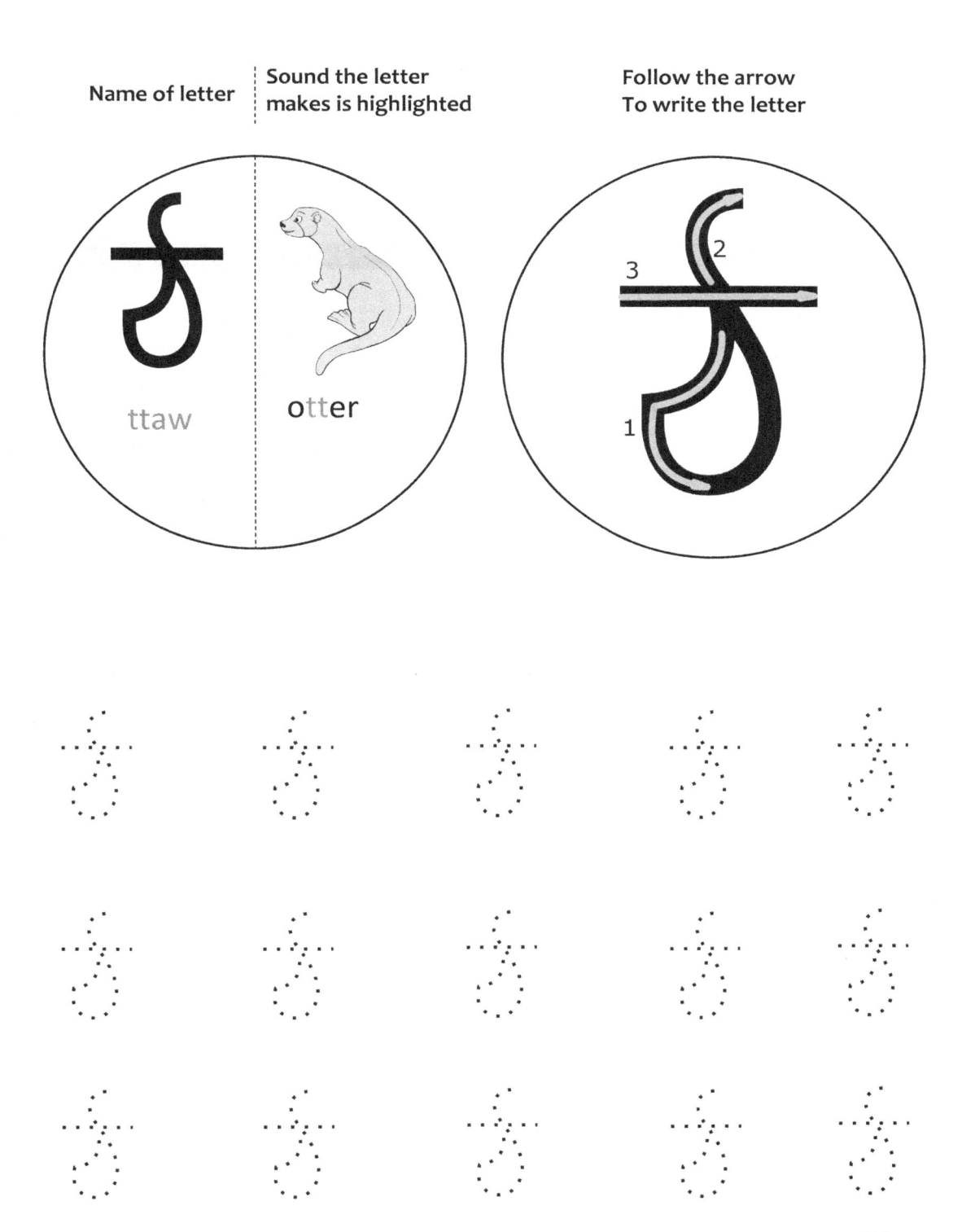

| Name of letter | Sound the letter makes is highlighted | Follow the arrow To write the letter |

daw | dinosaur

30

Name of letter	Sound the letter makes is highlighted	Follow the arrow To write the letter
ট dhaw	dhaka (capital of Bangladesh)	

| Name of letter | Sound the letter makes is highlighted | Follow the arrow To write the letter |

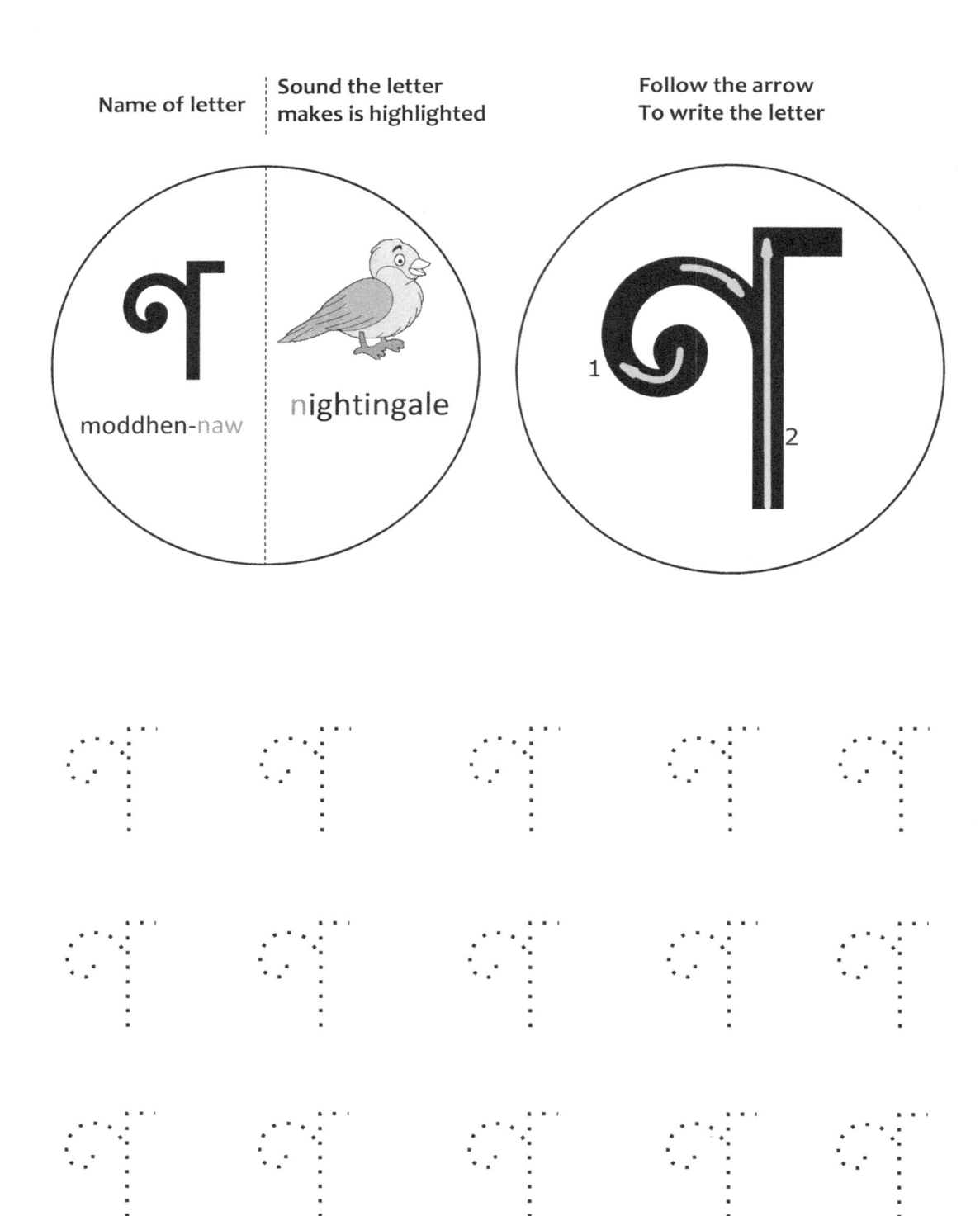

ণ

moddhen-naw

nightingale

32

Draw a line to connect each letter to it's name

ট	dhaw
ঠ	moddhen-naw
ড	daw
ঢ	taw
ণ	ttaw

With the top half of your tongue gently pressed against the top of your mouth, try to make the sound **taw**. The similar sound to **taw** that you made is the sound of the dental letter ত (**t̪aw**). Letter "t" with the dental symbol ̪ underneath it denotes the sound of the letter ত.

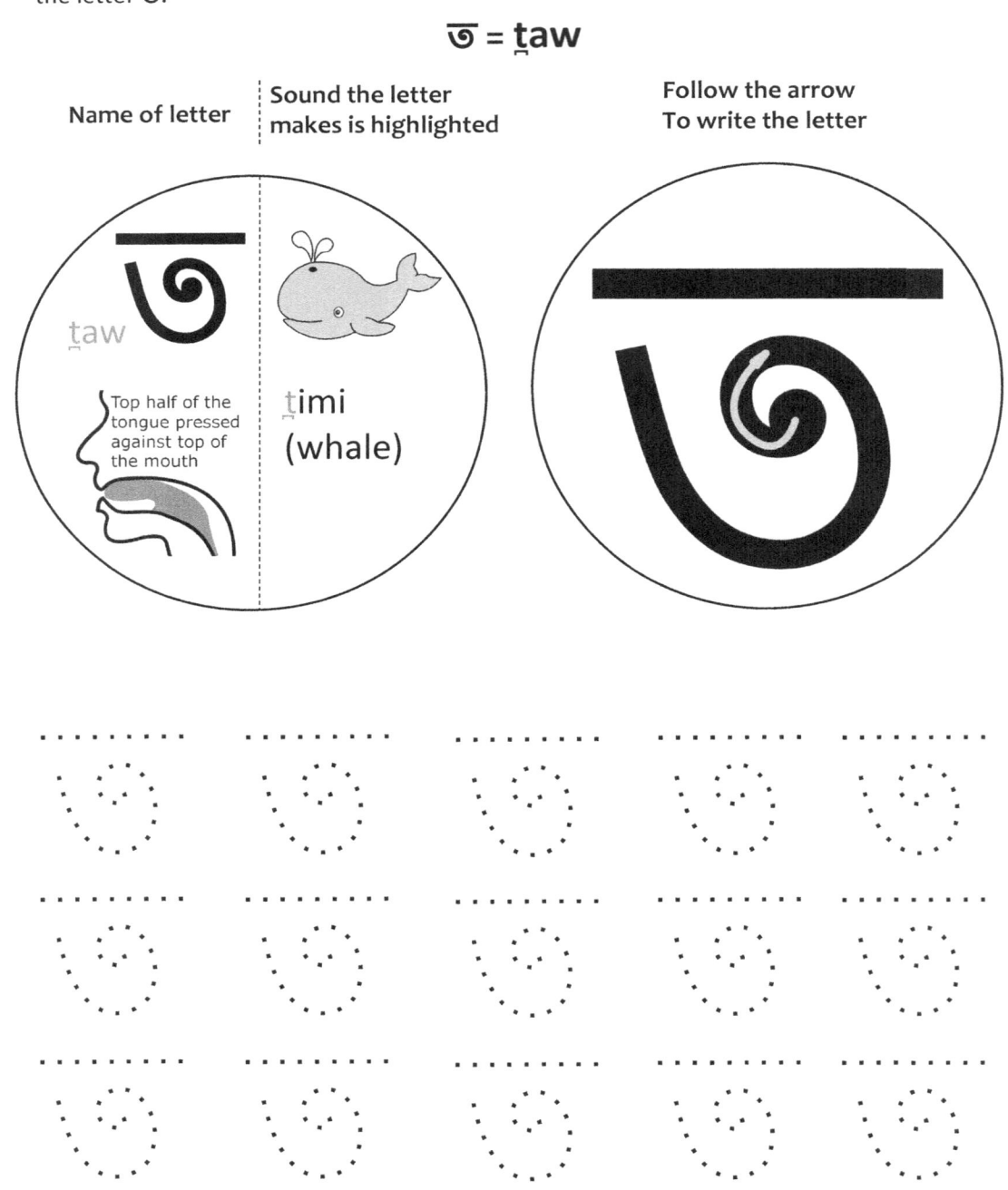

$$ত = t̪aw$$

Name of letter

Sound the letter makes is highlighted

Follow the arrow To write the letter

t̪aw

Top half of the tongue pressed against top of the mouth

t̪imi (whale)

The previous dental letter ত (ṯaw) with the added "h" sound makes the sound of this dental letter থ (**ṯhaw**).

থ = ṯhaw

Name of letter | **Sound the letter makes is highlighted** | **Follow the arrow To write the letter**

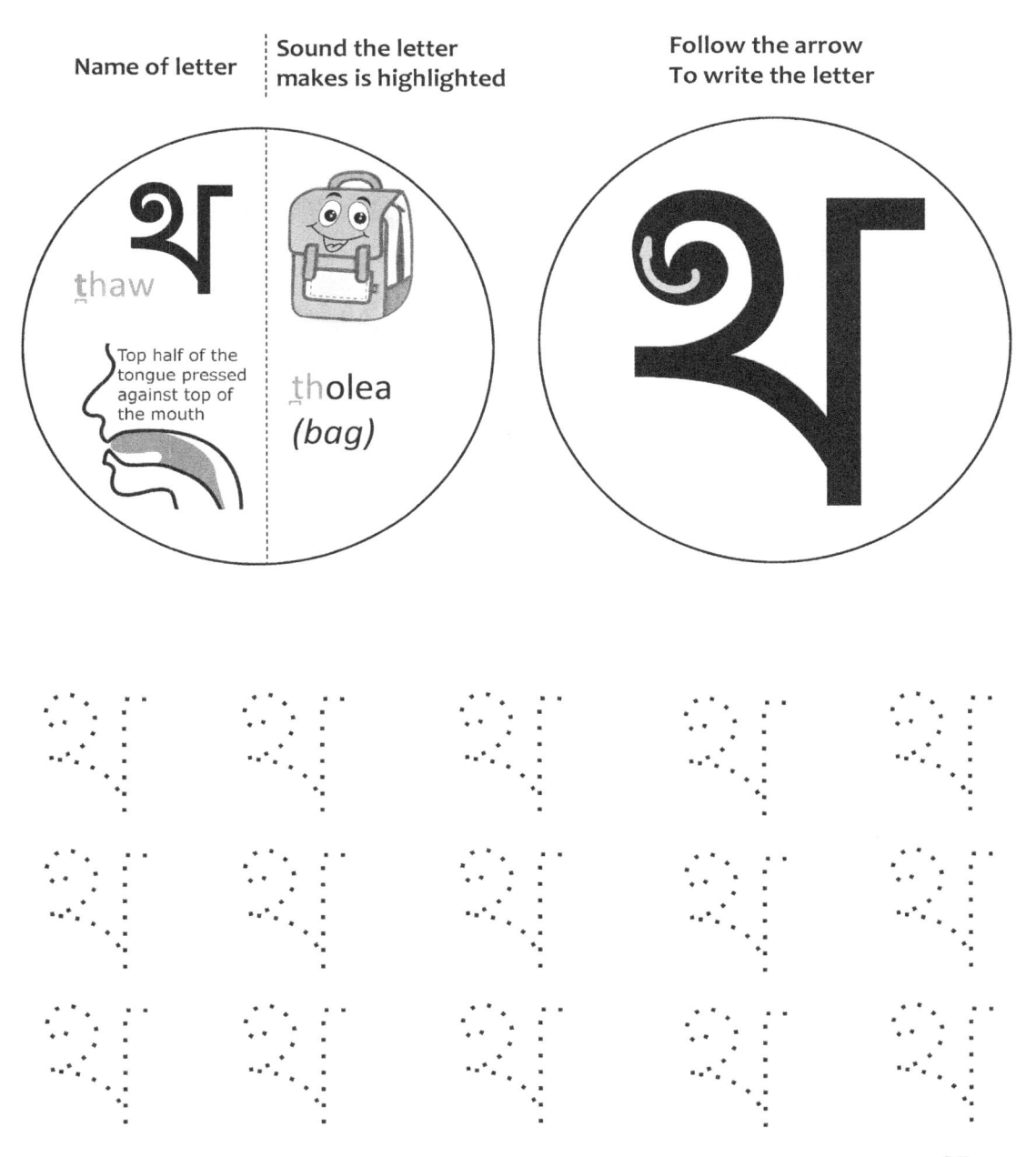

ṯhaw

Top half of the tongue pressed against top of the mouth

ṯholea
(bag)

35

With the top half of your tongue gently pressed against the top of your mouth, try to make the sound **daw.** The similar sound to **daw** that you made is the sound of the dental letter দ (**daw**). Letter "d" with the dental symbol ̣ underneath it denotes the sound of the letter দ.

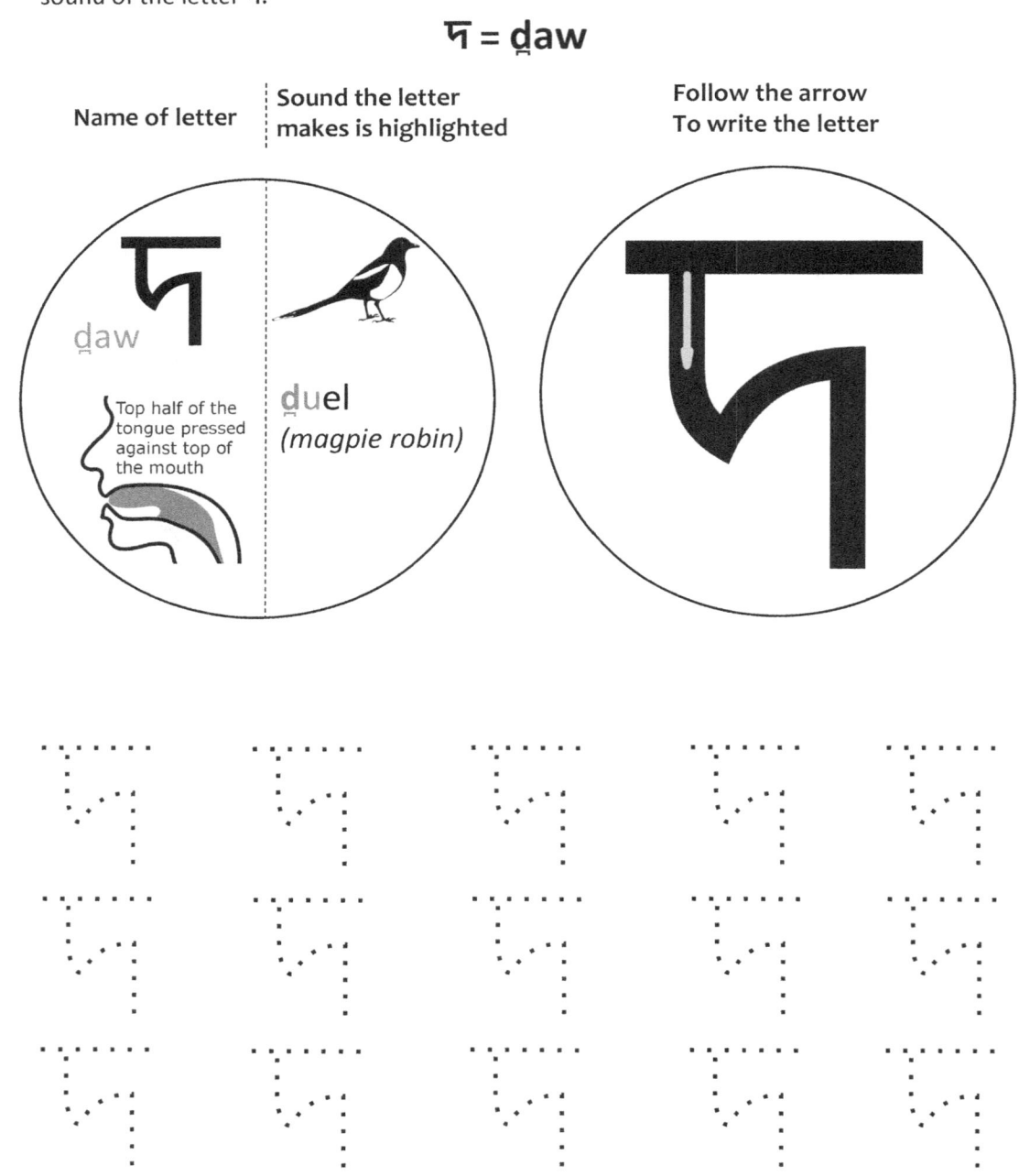

দ = d̠aw

Name of letter | **Sound the letter makes is highlighted** | **Follow the arrow To write the letter**

d̠aw

Top half of the tongue pressed against top of the mouth

d̠uel
(magpie robin)

36

The previous dental letter দ (daw) with the added "h" sound makes the sound of this dental letter ধ (dhaw).

ধ = dhaw

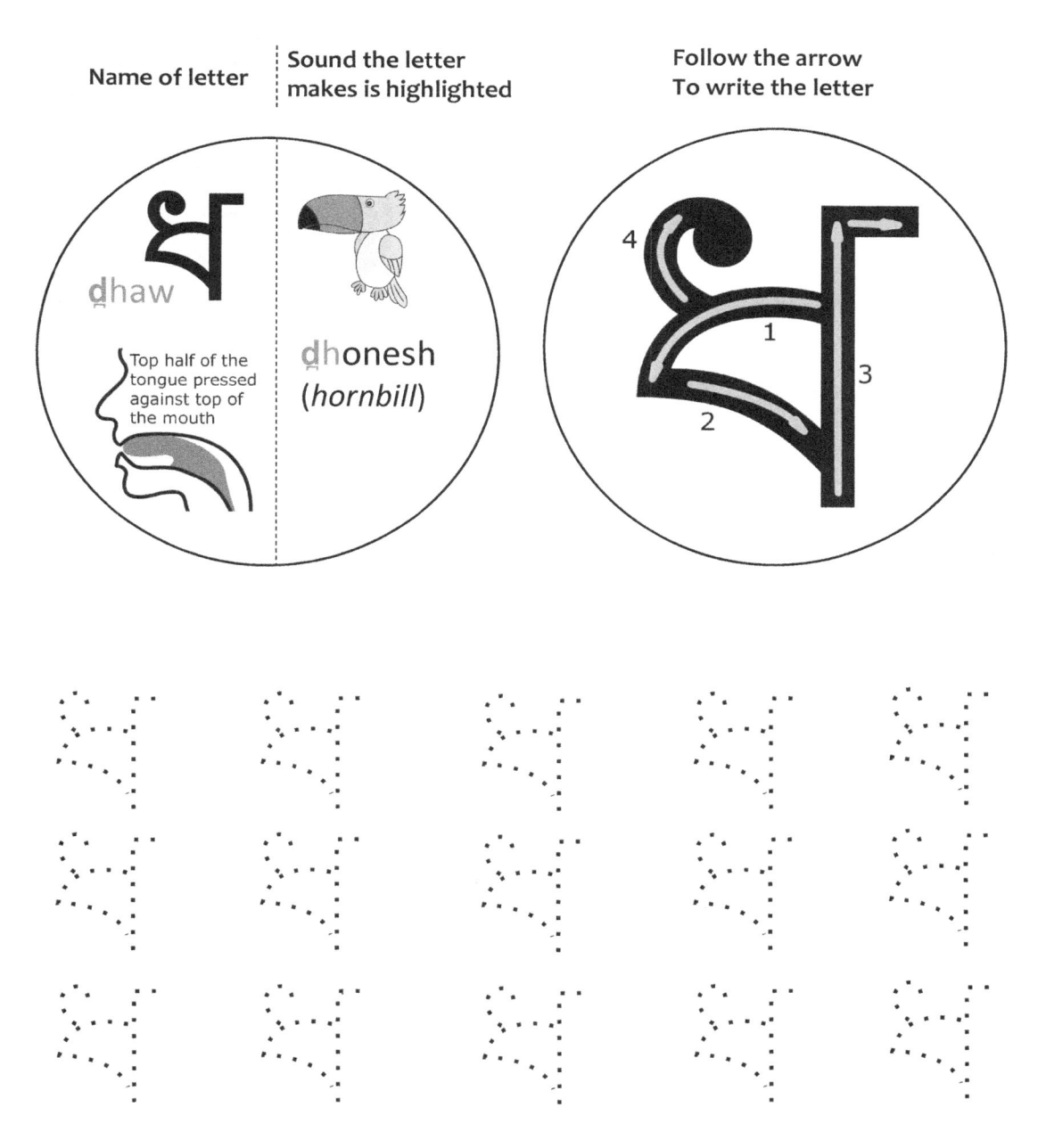

Name of letter

Sound the letter makes is highlighted

Follow the arrow To write the letter

dhaw

Top half of the tongue pressed against top of the mouth

dhonesh (*hornbill*)

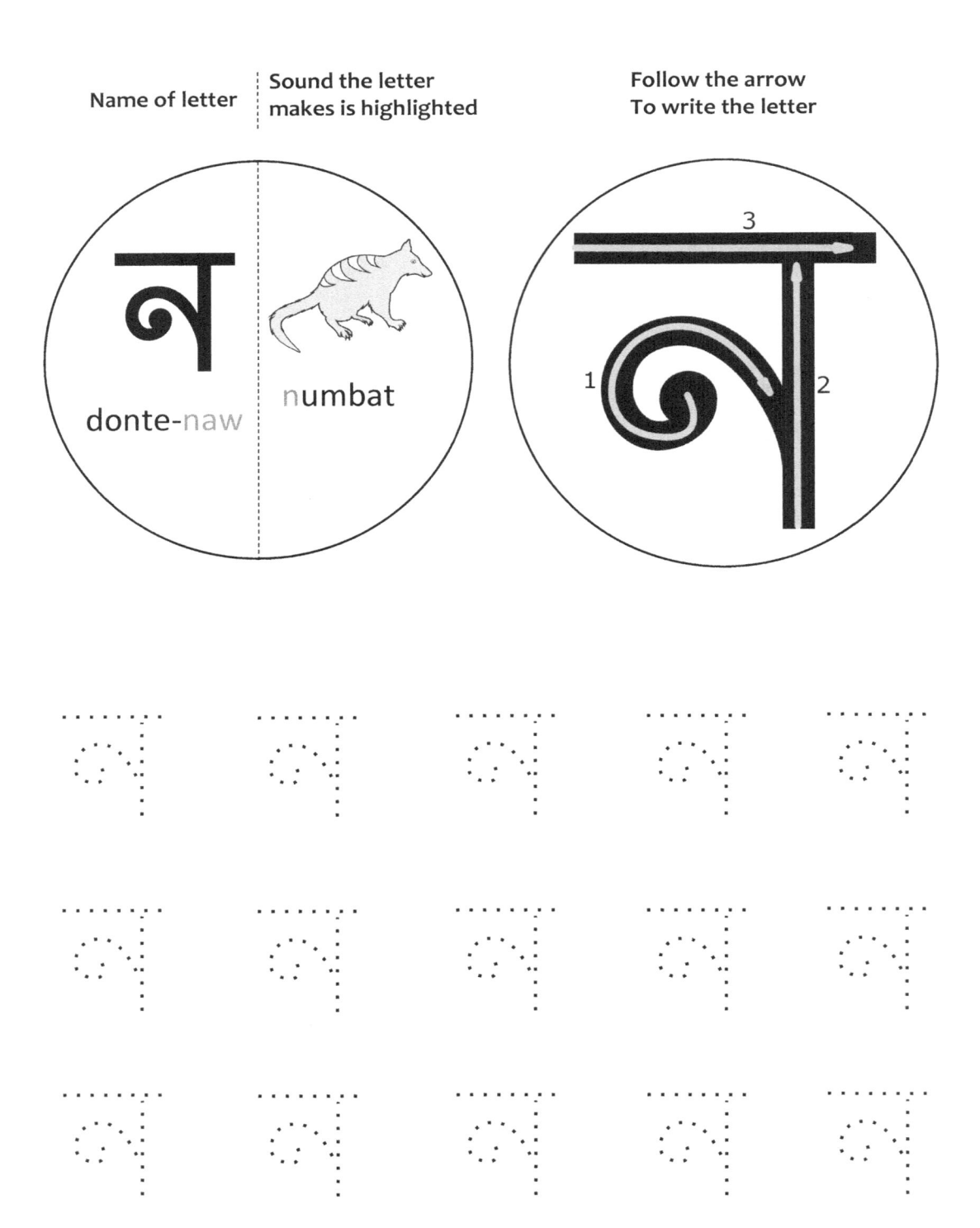

Name of letter | Sound the letter makes is highlighted | Follow the arrow To write the letter

ন
donte-naw | numbat

38

Draw a line to connect each letter to it's name

ত	d̪aw
থ	d̪haw
দ	t̪haw
ধ	t̪aw
ন	donte-naw

| Name of letter | Sound the letter makes is highlighted | Follow the arrow To write the letter |

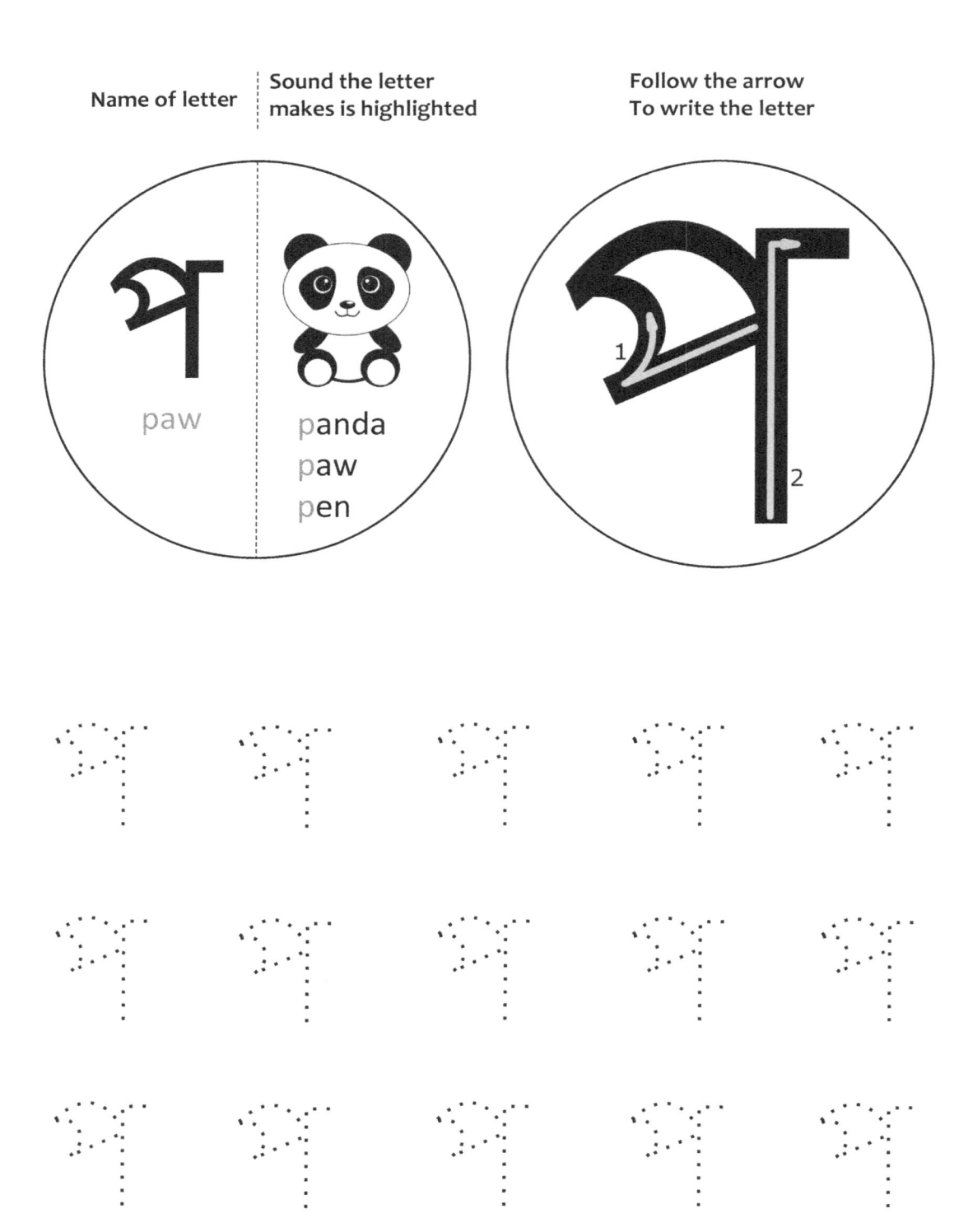

প   paw

panda
paw
pen

40

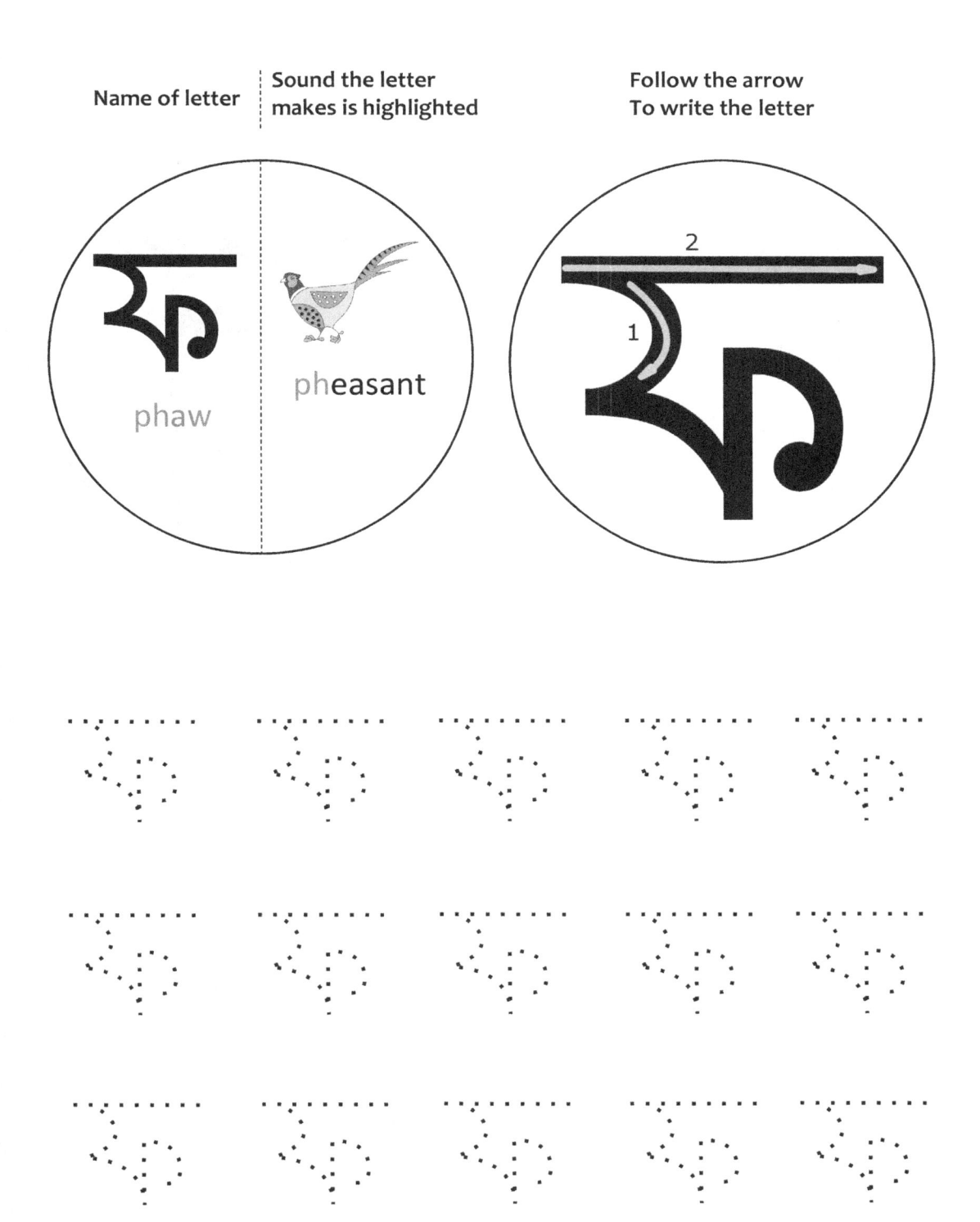

Name of letter	Sound the letter makes is highlighted	Follow the arrow To write the letter
phaw	**ph**easant	

41

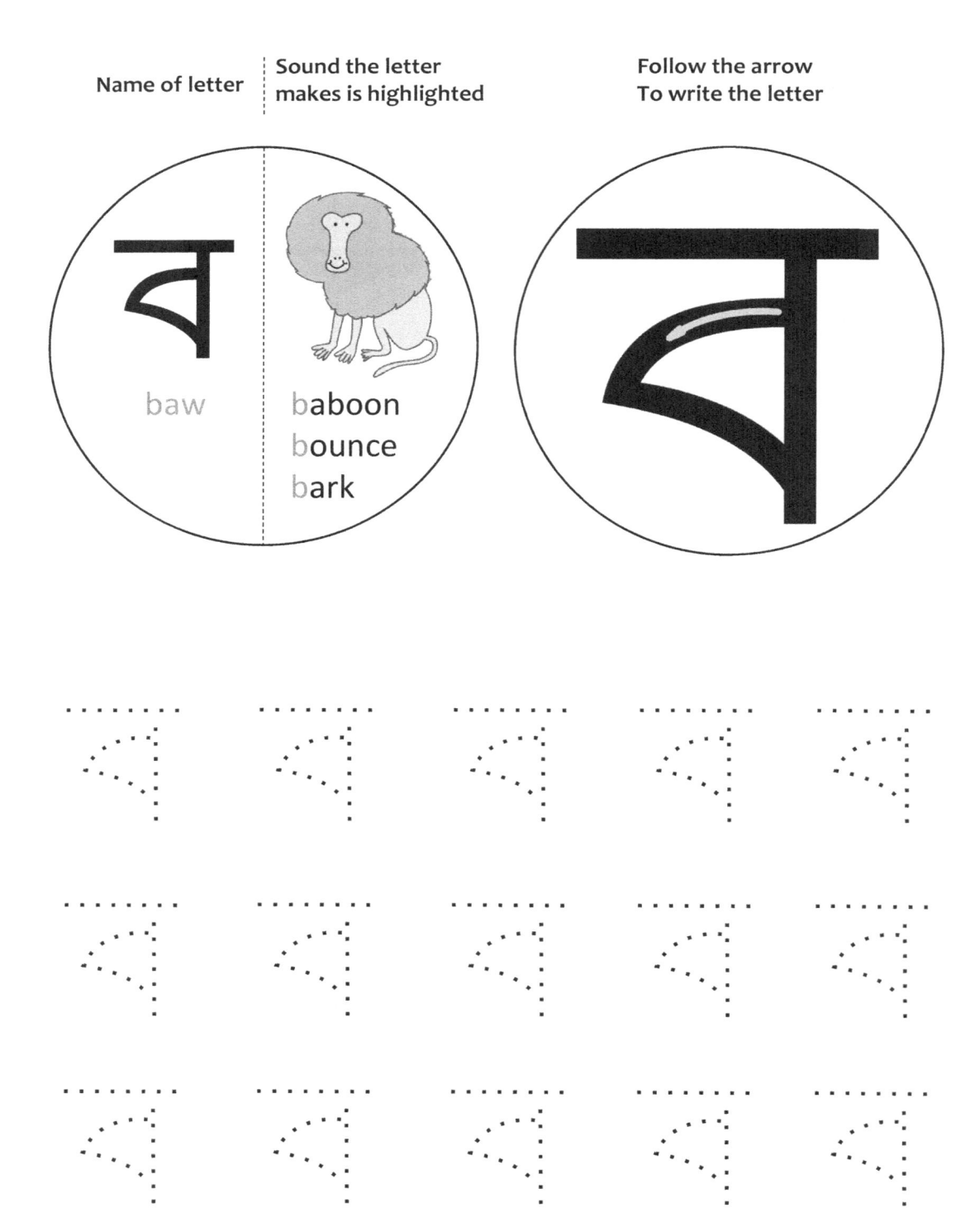

Name of letter | Sound the letter makes is highlighted

Follow the arrow
To write the letter

ব

baw

baboon
bounce
bark

42

| Name of letter | Sound the letter makes is highlighted | Follow the arrow To write the letter |

bhaw | bhai (brother)

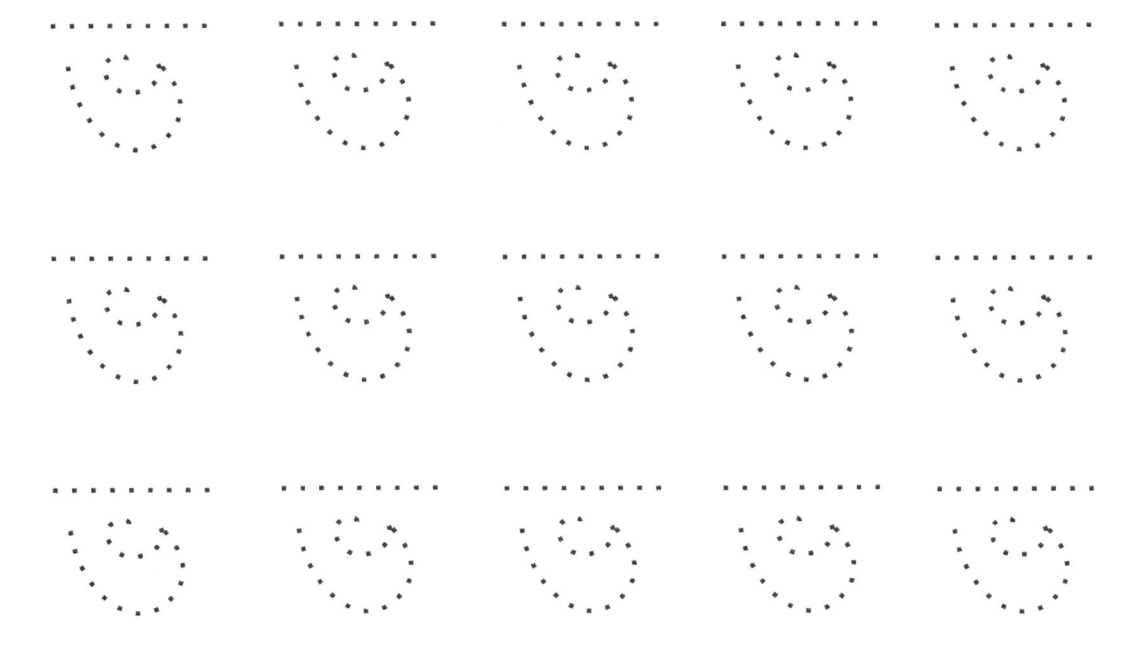

43

Name of letter	Sound the letter makes is highlighted	Follow the arrow To write the letter
ম	**m**anta ray **m**uffin **m**ay	
maw		

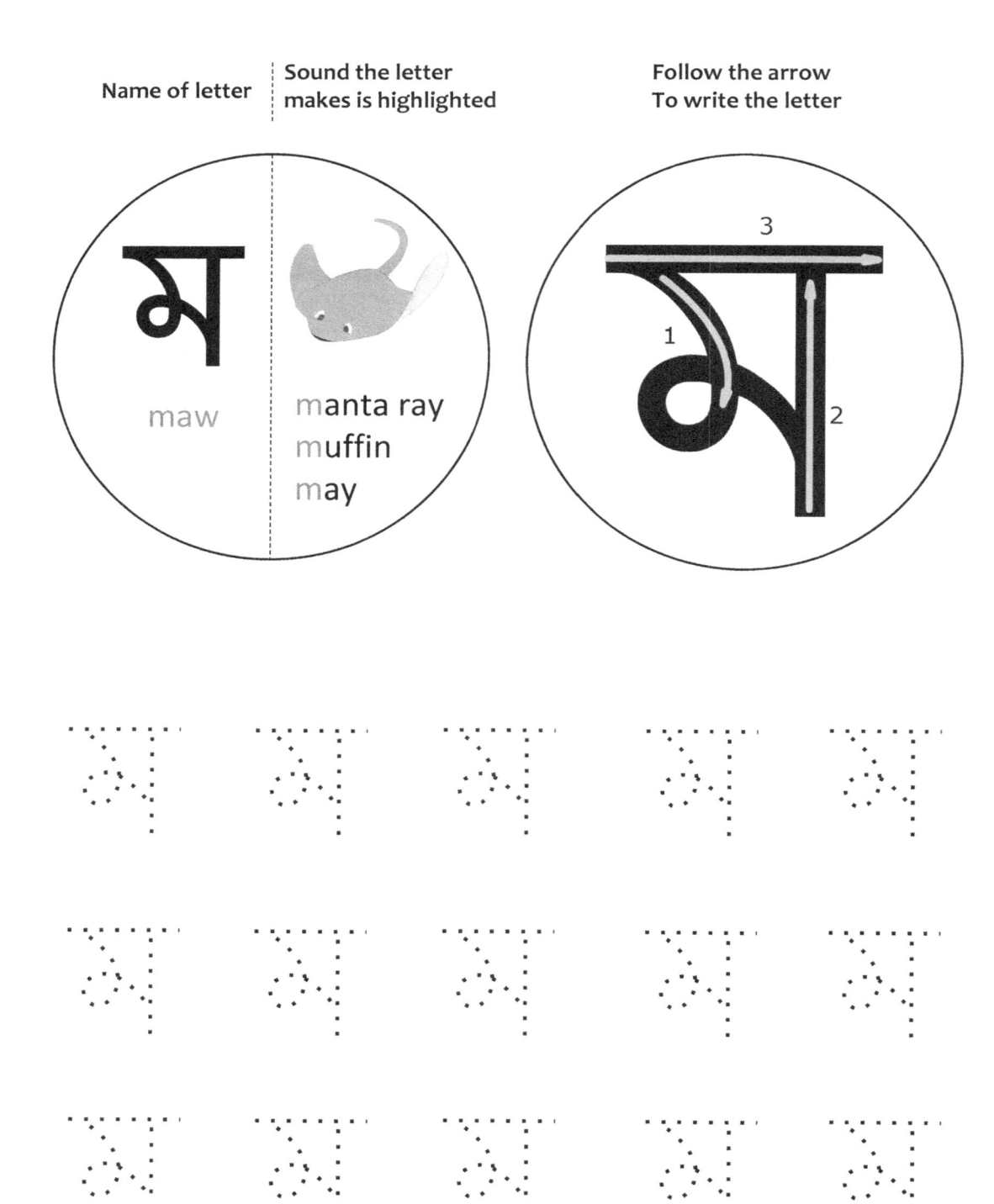

44

Draw a line to connect each letter to it's name

প	paw
ফ	maw
ব	phaw
ভ	baw
ম	bhaw

Name of letter	Sound the letter makes is highlighted	Follow the arrow To write the letter

ontesto-jaw

jaguar
jug
jam

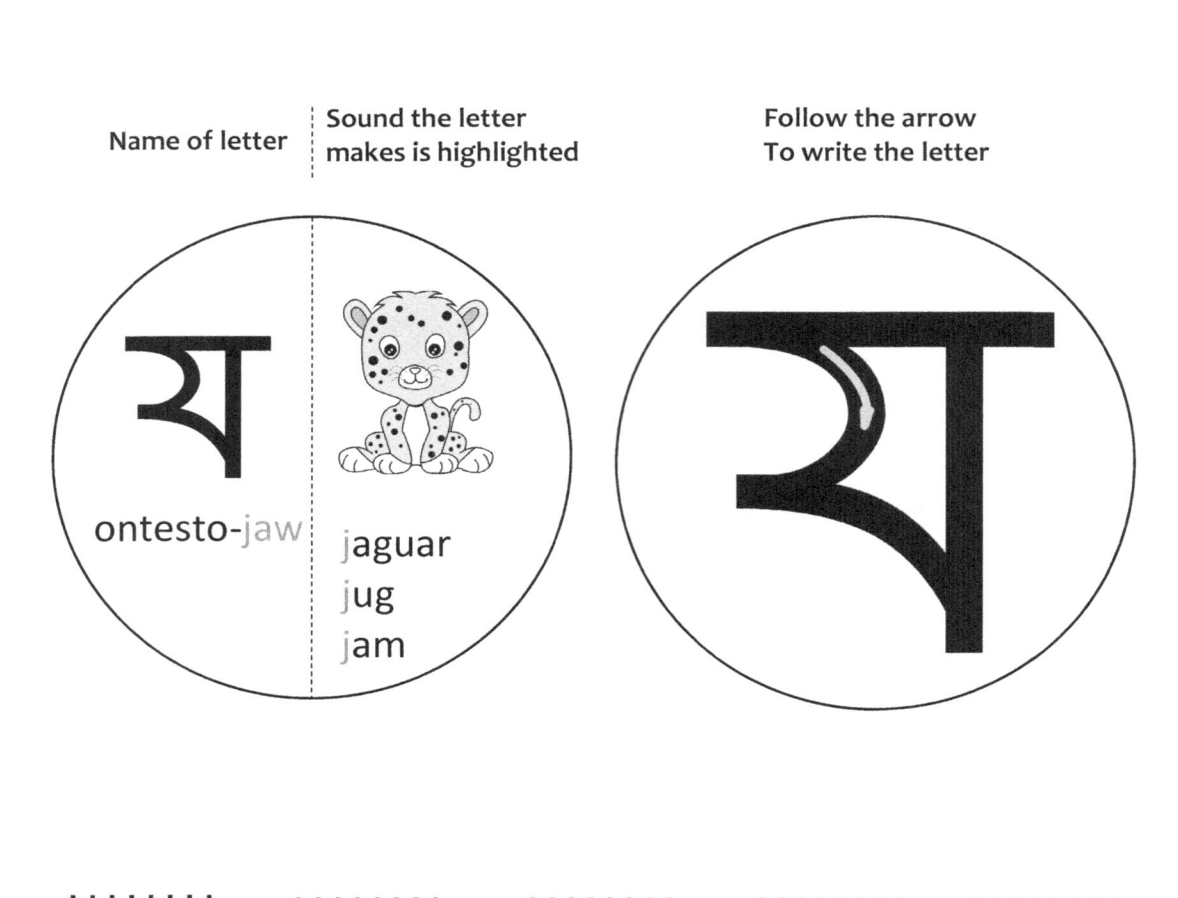

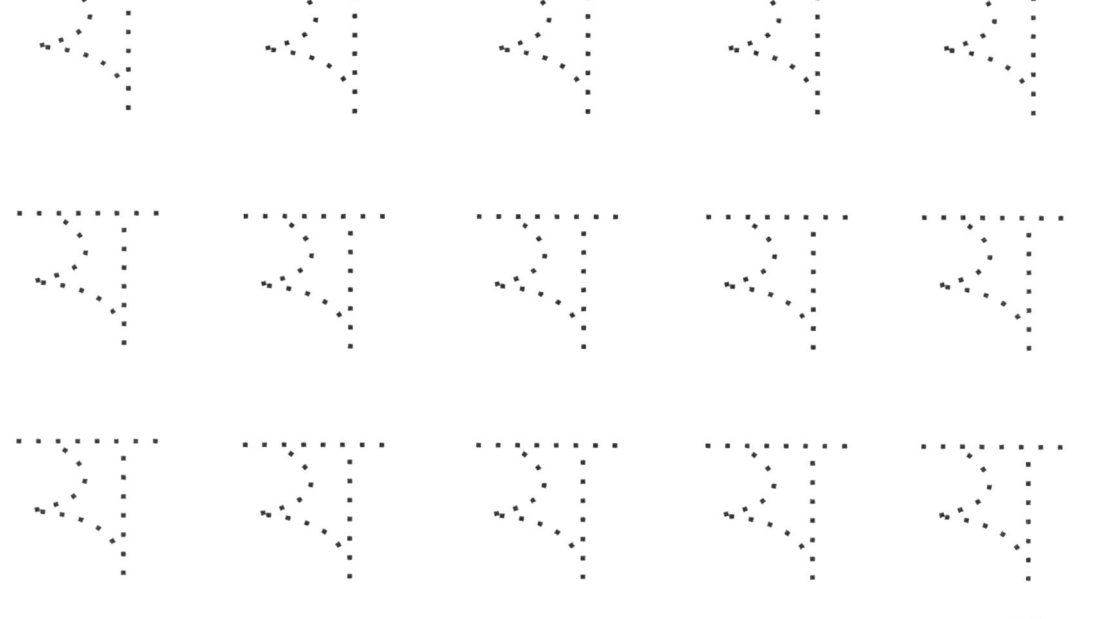

Name of letter	Sound the letter makes is highlighted	Follow the arrow To write the letter
raw — Tip of toungue just behind the top front teeth	ho**r**in (deer)	

47

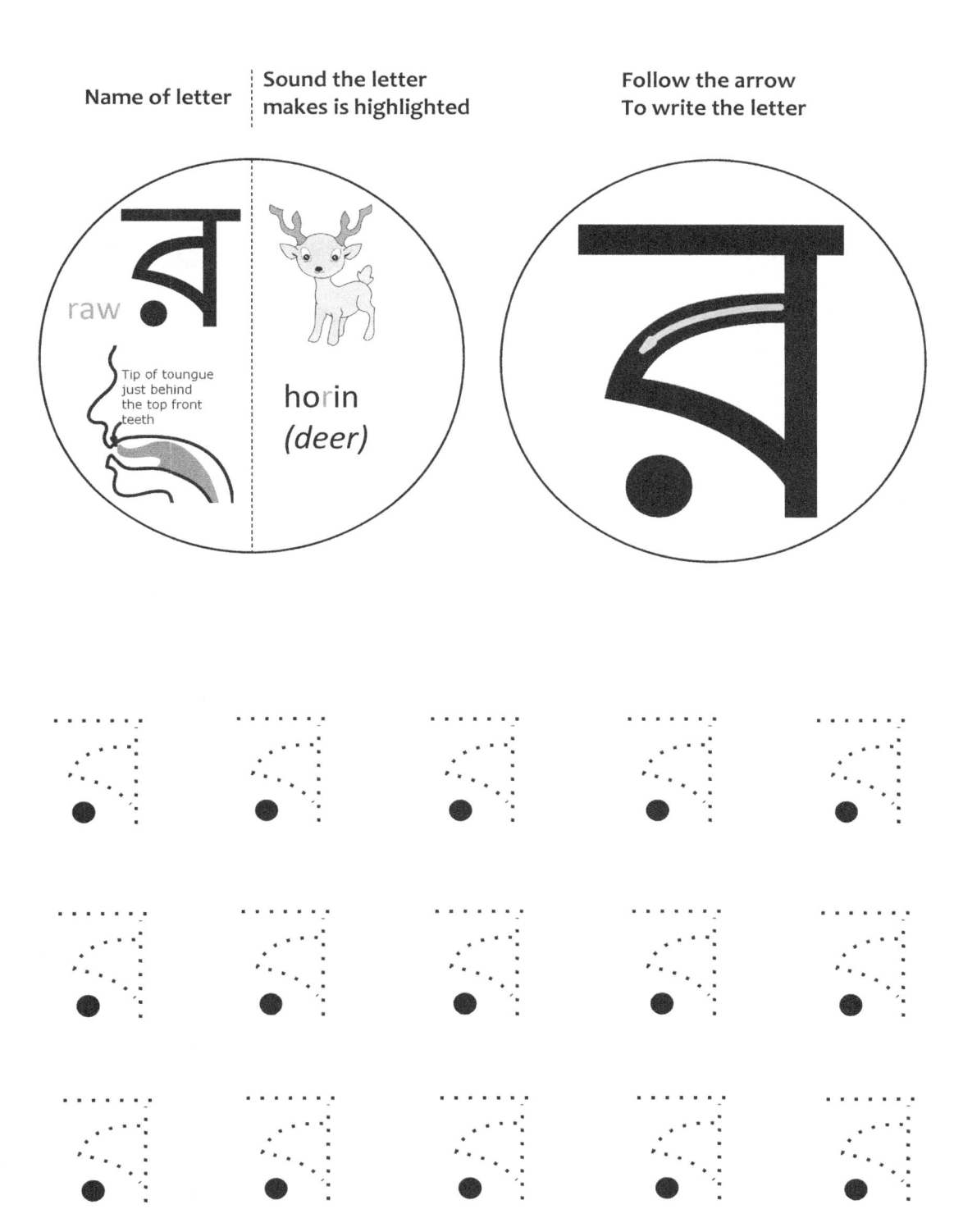

Name of letter | **Sound the letter makes is highlighted** | **Follow the arrow To write the letter**

ल

law

lamb
lion
lock

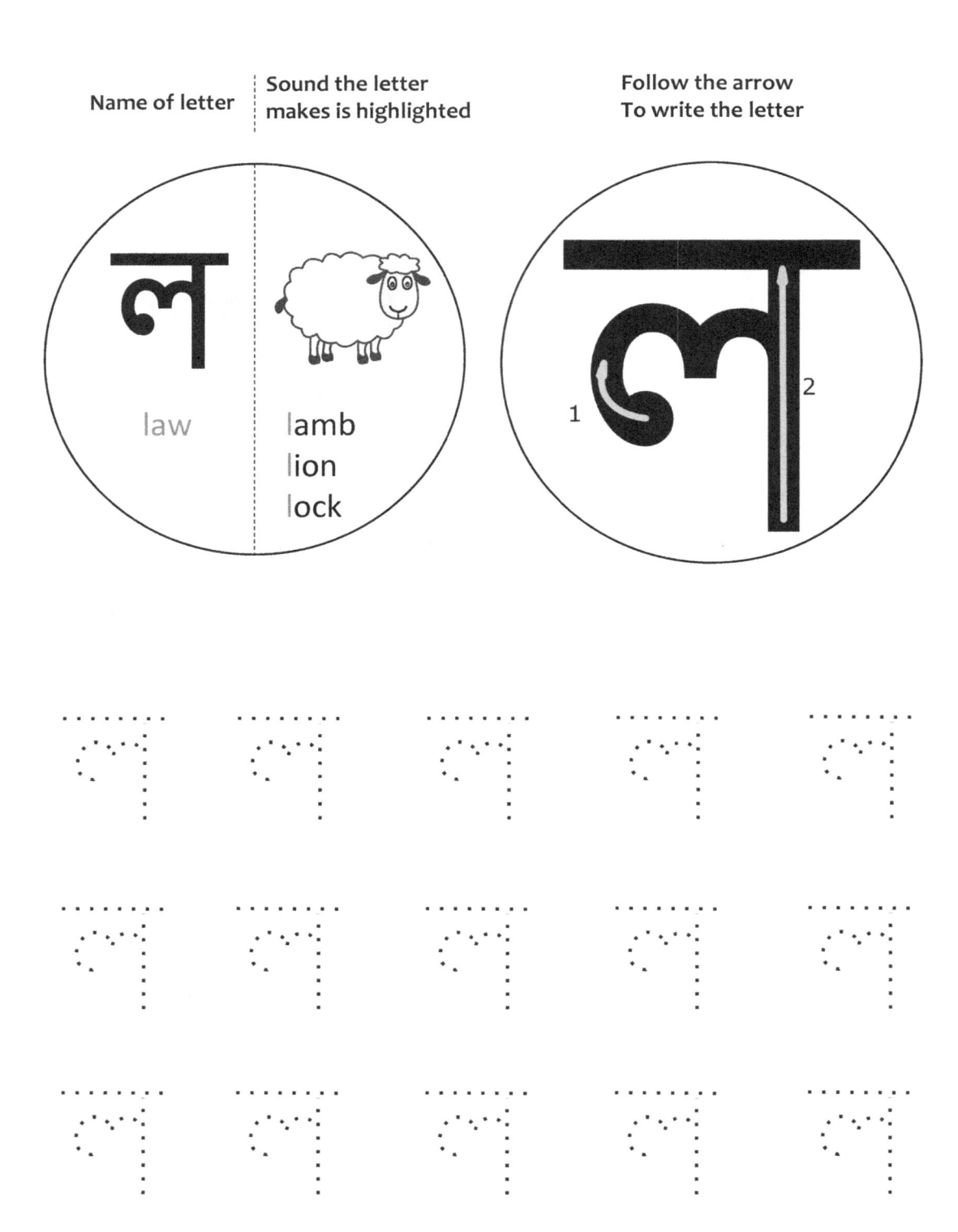

48

| Name of letter | Sound the letter makes is highlighted | Follow the arrow To write the letter |

শ

talibo-shaw | shark

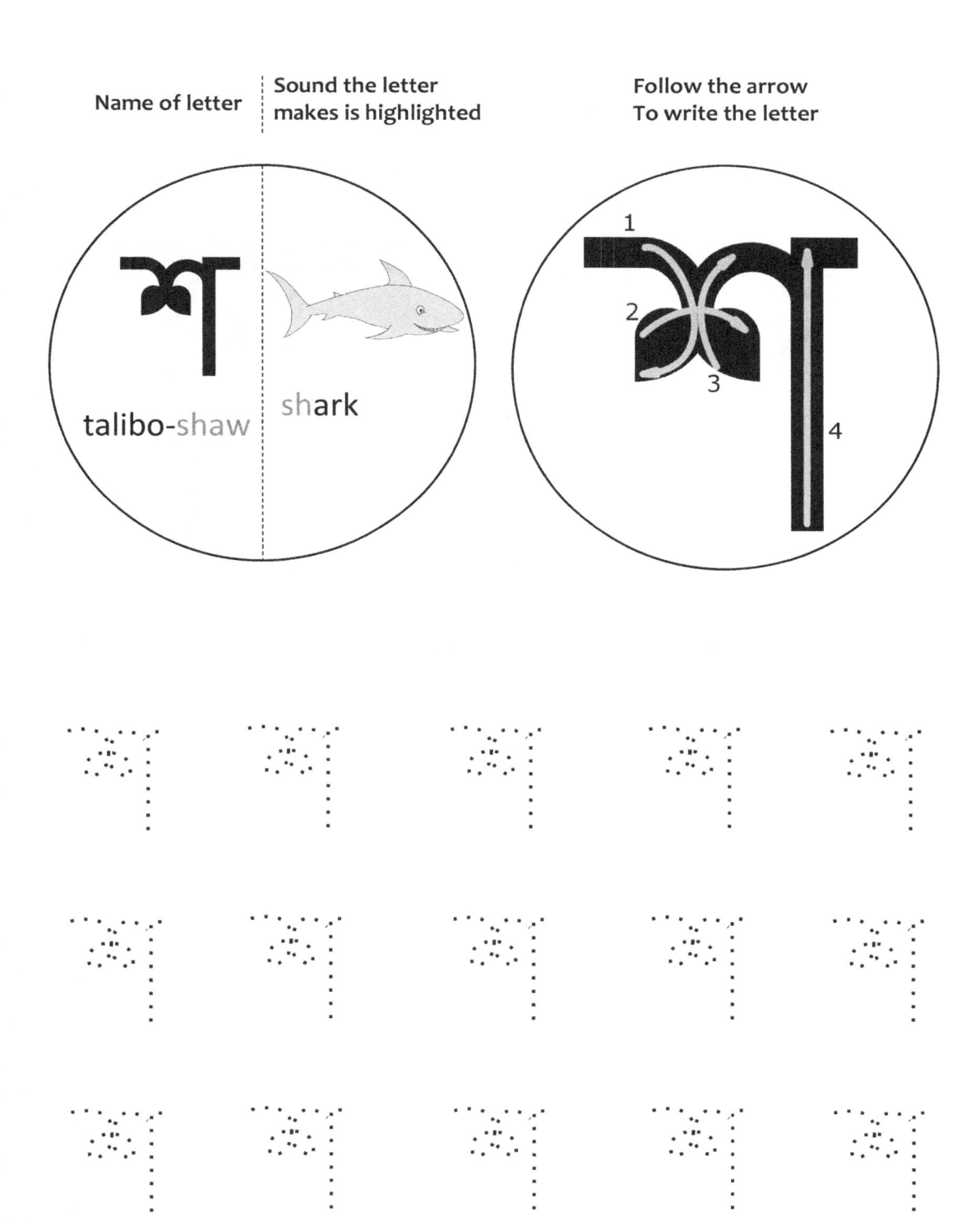

| Name of letter | Sound the letter makes is highlighted | Follow the arrow To write the letter |

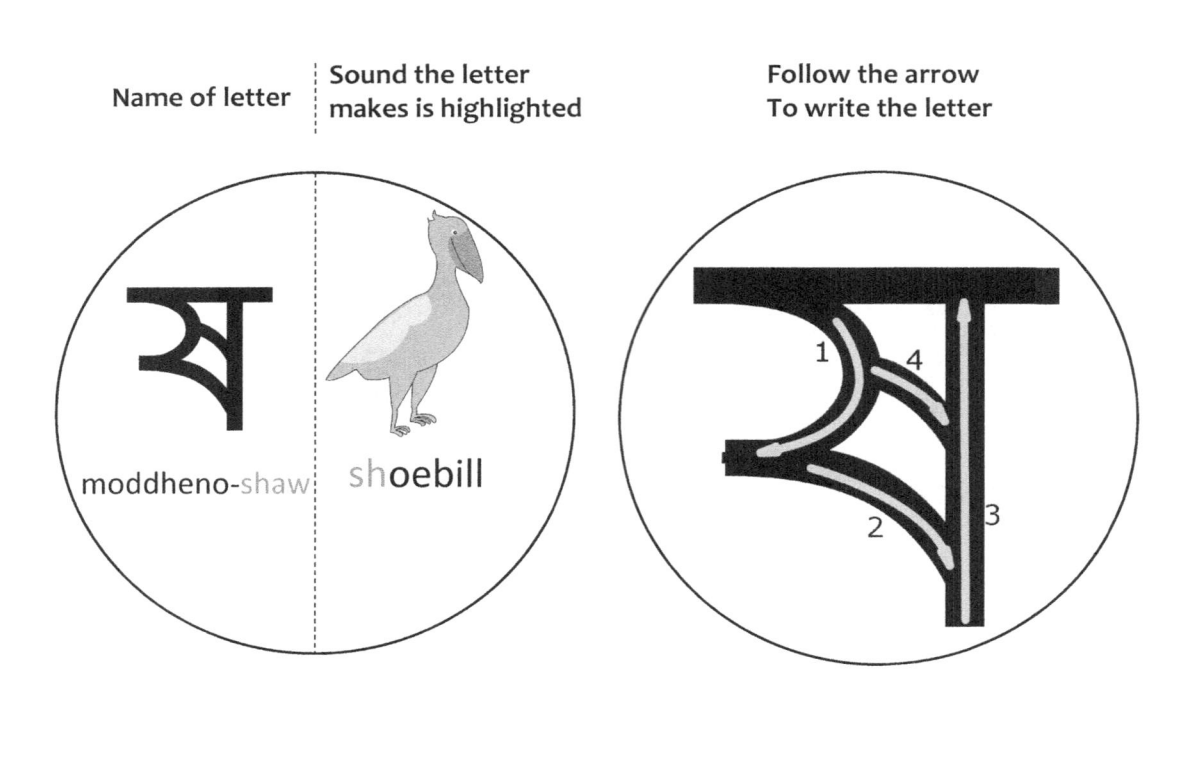

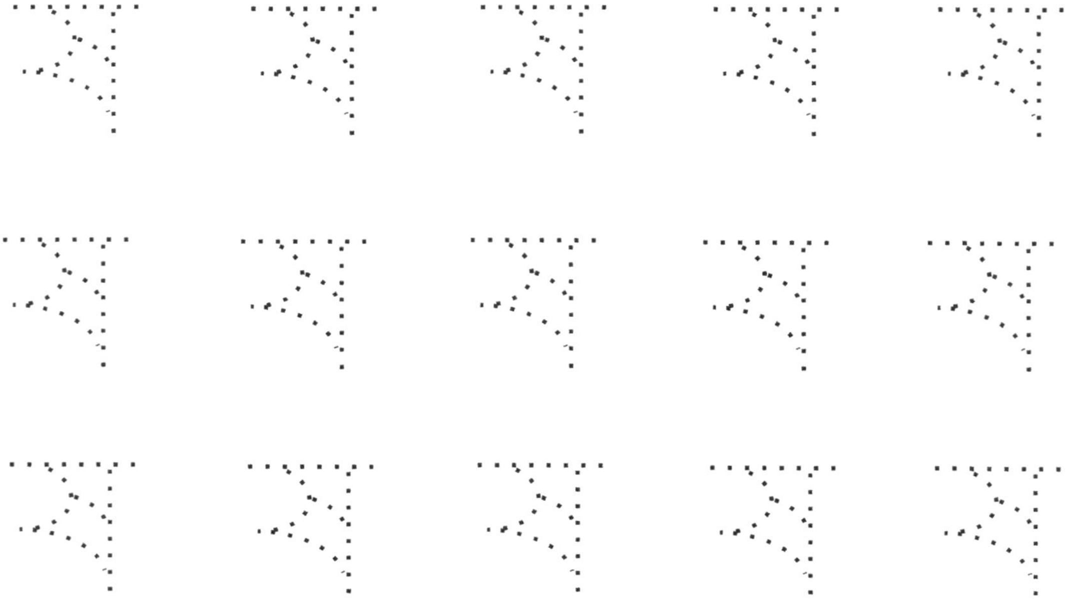

moddheno-shaw | **sh**oebill

50

Name of letter | Sound the letter makes is highlighted | Follow the arrow To write the letter

স

donte-shaw
(makes s or sh sound)

skunk
sheep

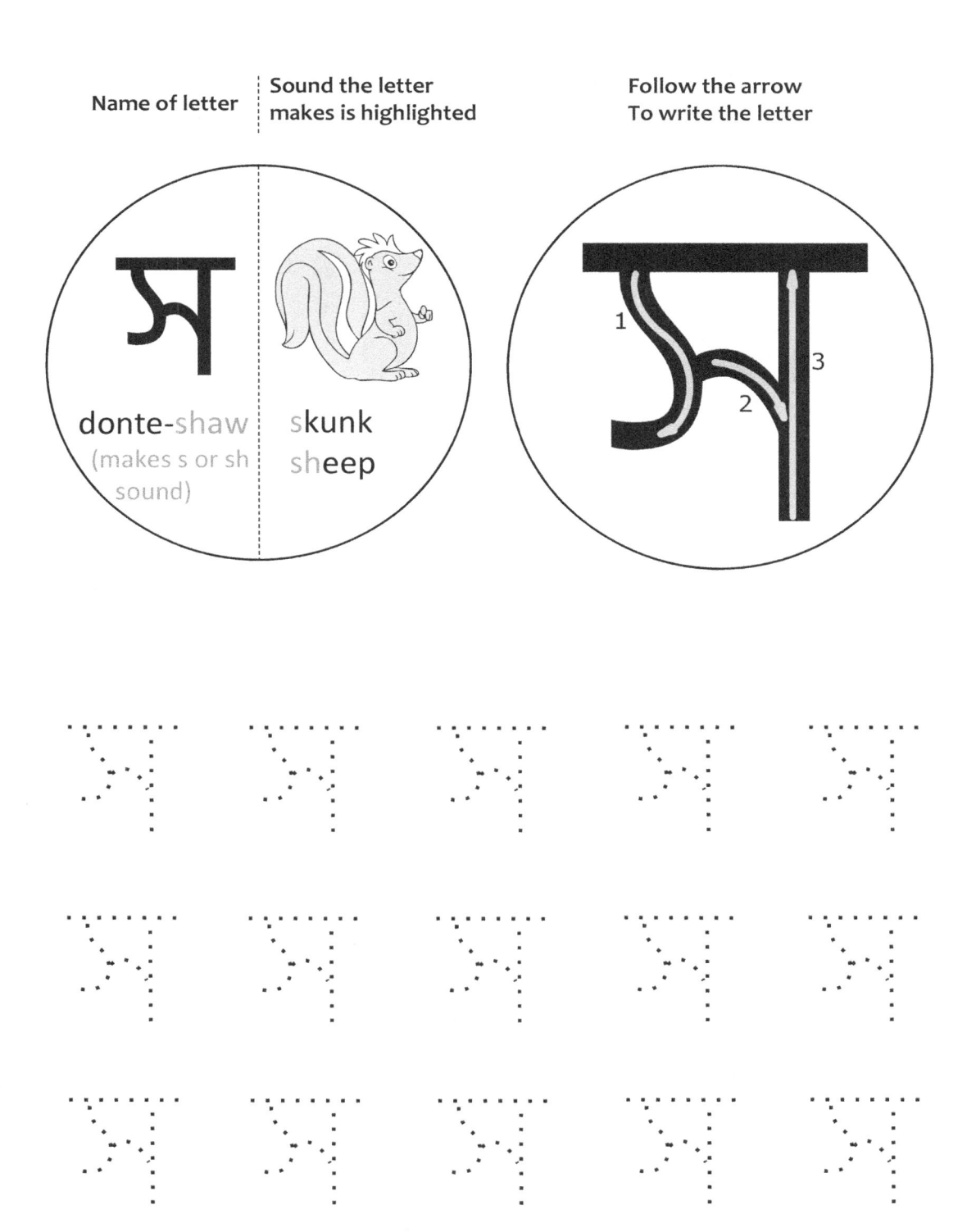

51

Draw a line to connect each letter to it's name

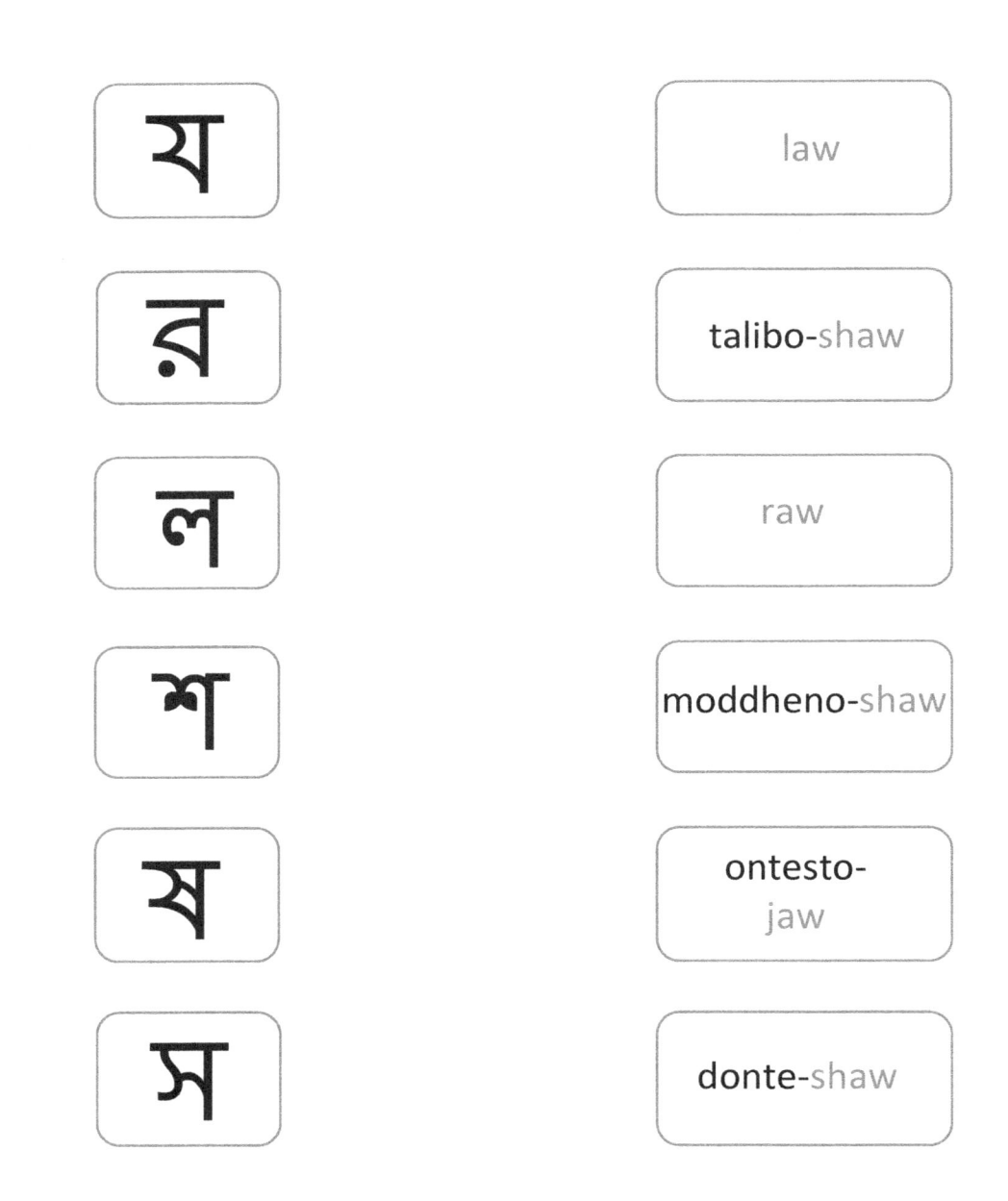

য	law
র	talibo-shaw
ল	raw
শ	moddheno-shaw
ষ	ontesto-jaw
স	donte-shaw

Name of letter | Sound the letter makes is highlighted

Follow the arrow
To write the letter

ह
haw

groundhog
house
hut

53

| Name of letter | Sound the letter makes is highlighted | Follow the arrow To write the letter |

ড়

doya-shunno-raw

racoon
river
run

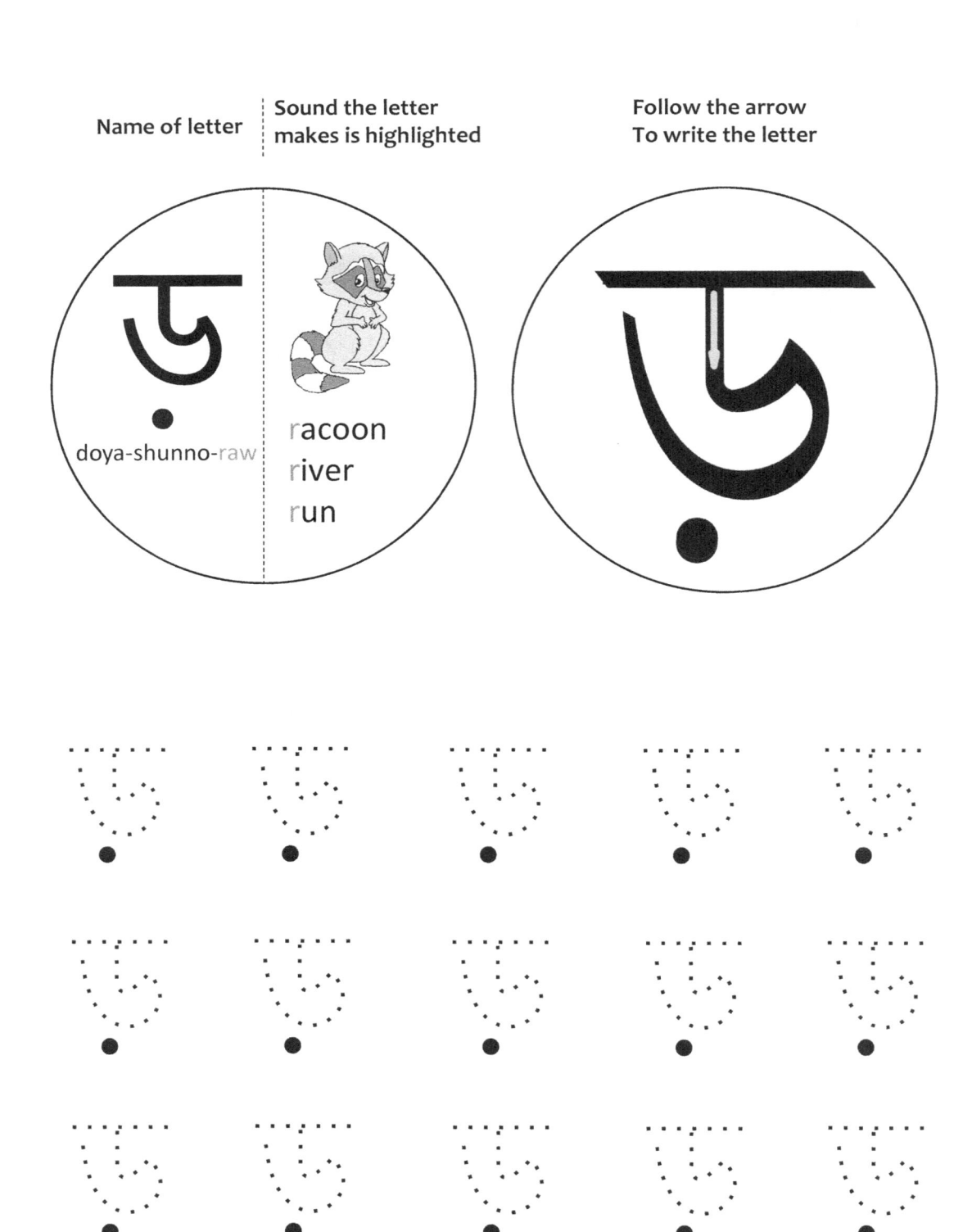

54

| Name of letter | Sound the letter makes is highlighted | Follow the arrow To write the letter |

ড়
dhoya-shunno-raw

borsha
(rainy season in Bangladesh)

55

| Name of letter | Sound the letter makes is highlighted | Follow the arrow To write the letter |

ontesto-aw | yak

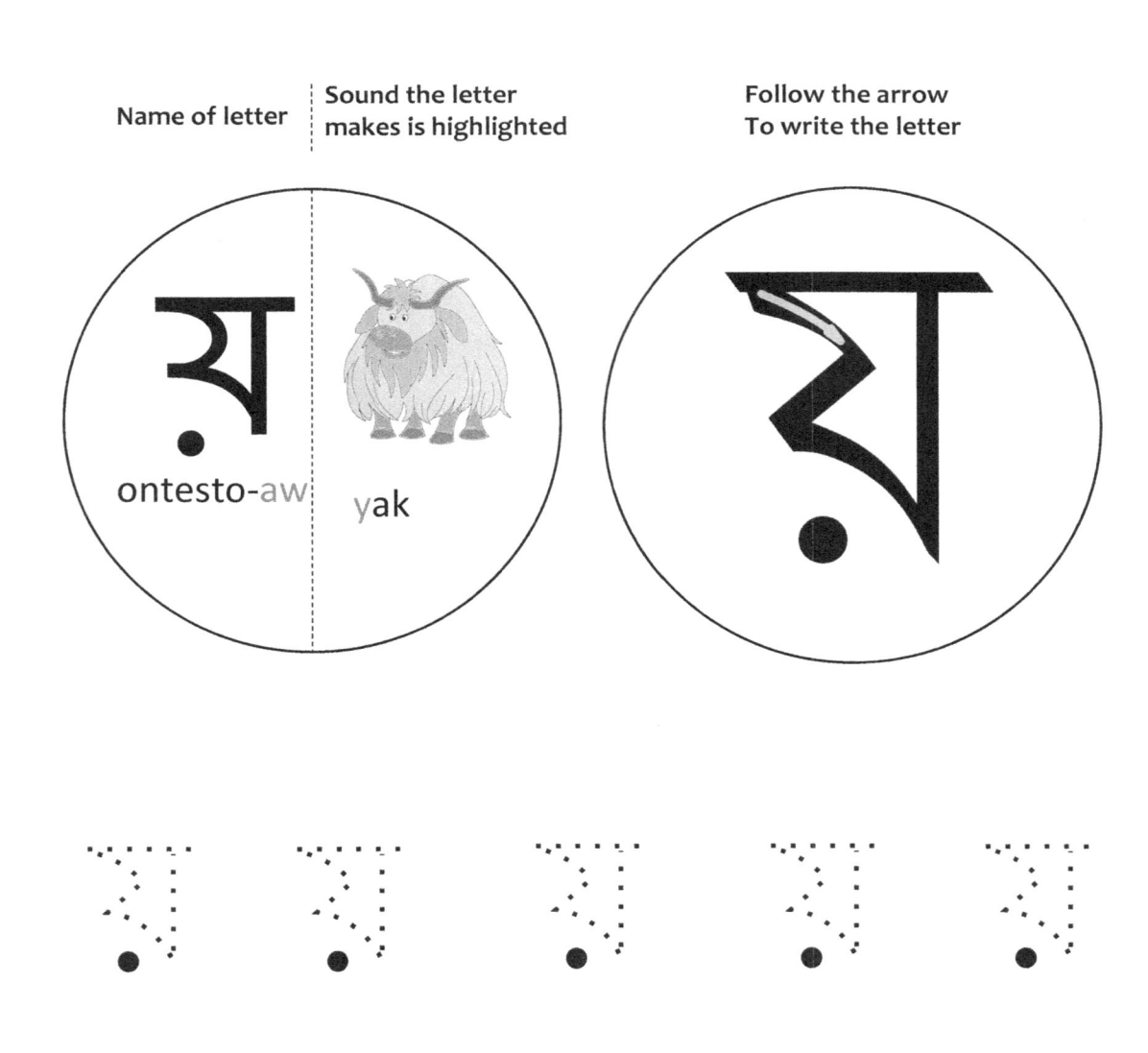

A variant form of the letter ত (ṯaw). It makes a short ত sound.

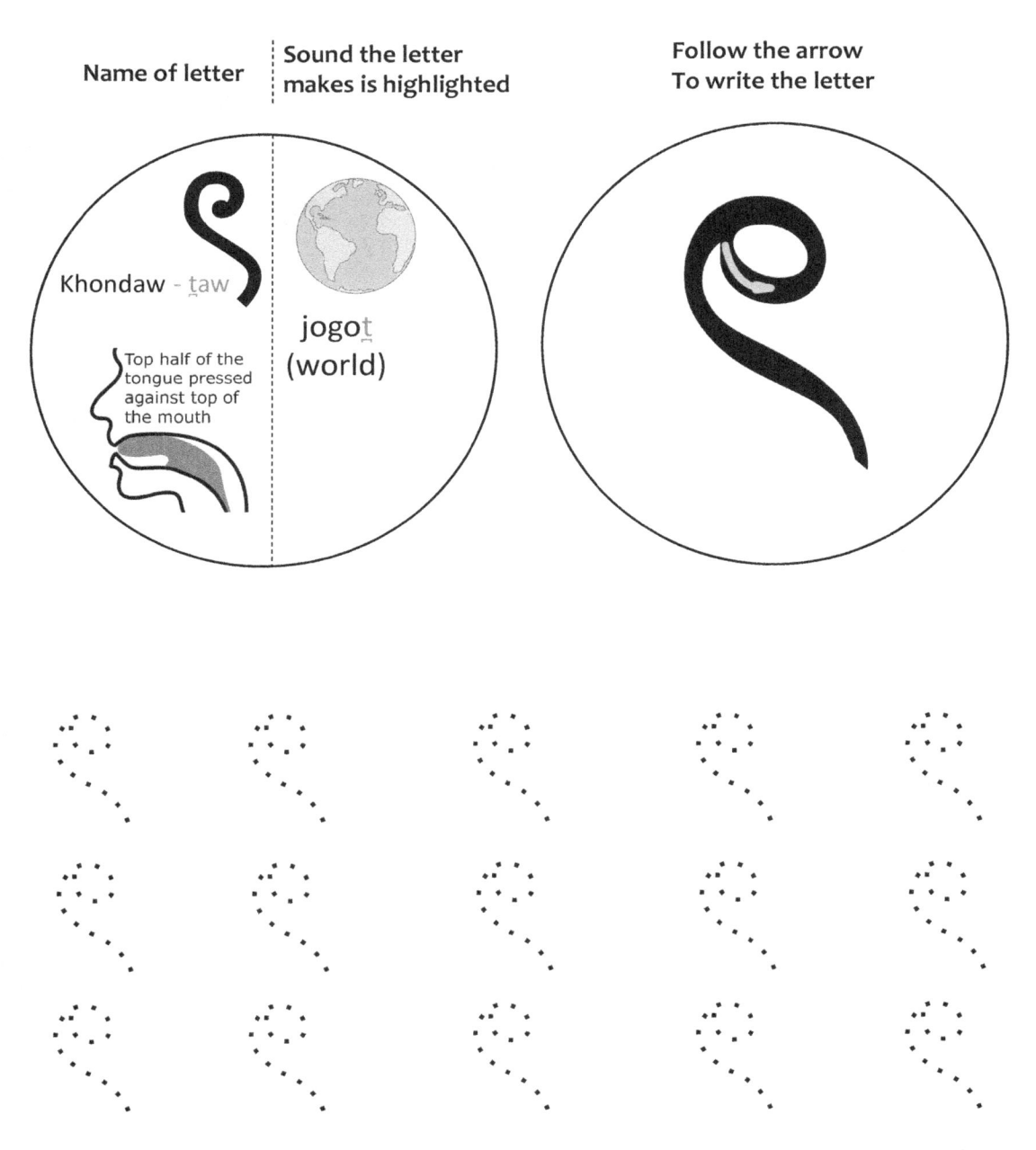

Name of letter | **Sound the letter makes is highlighted**

Khondaw - ṯaw

Top half of the tongue pressed against top of the mouth

jogoṯ (world)

Follow the arrow To write the letter

57

Name of letter	Sound the letter makes is highlighted	Follow the arrow To write the letter
Onush-shar	ba**ng**ladesh	

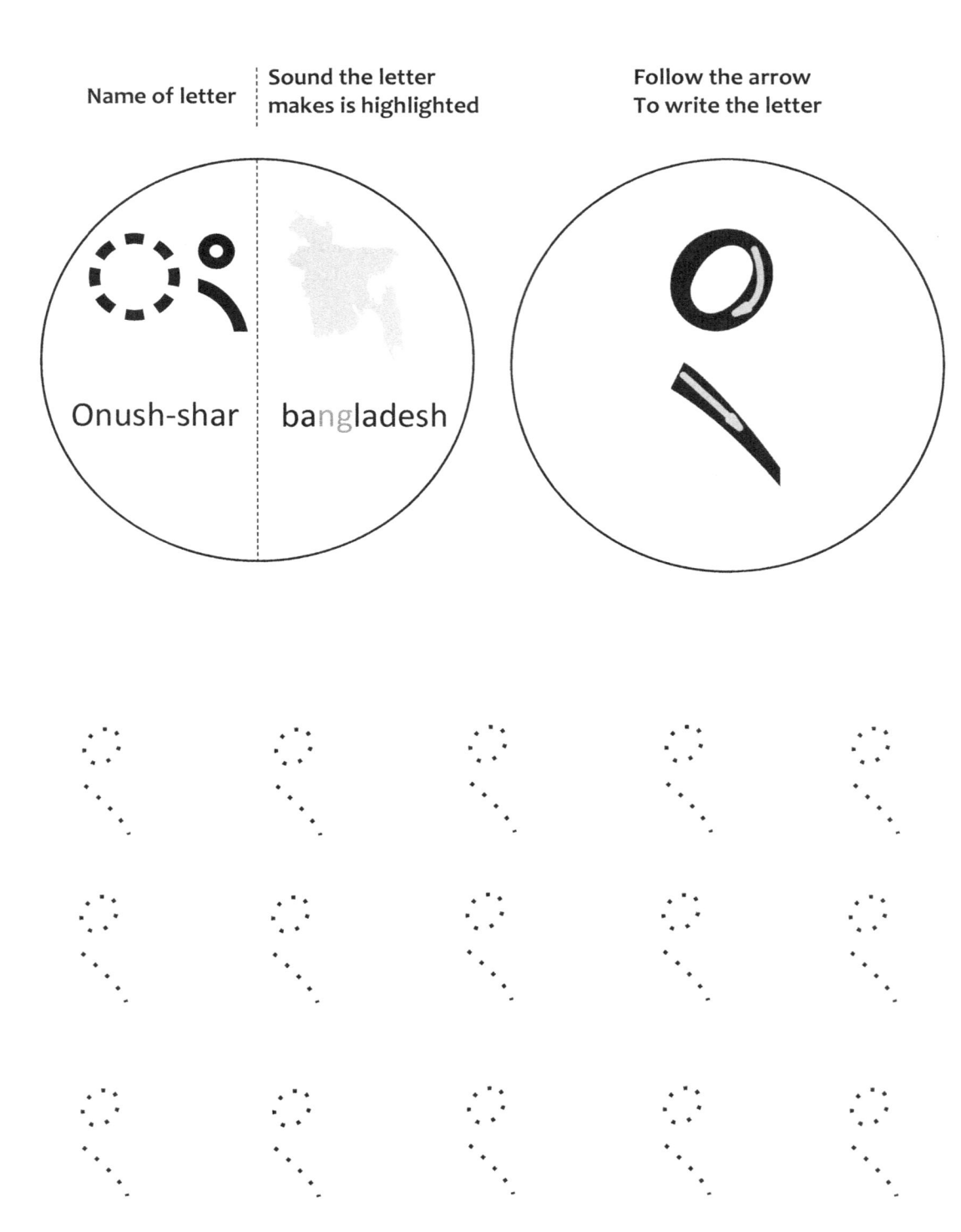

58

Draw a line to connect each letter to it's name

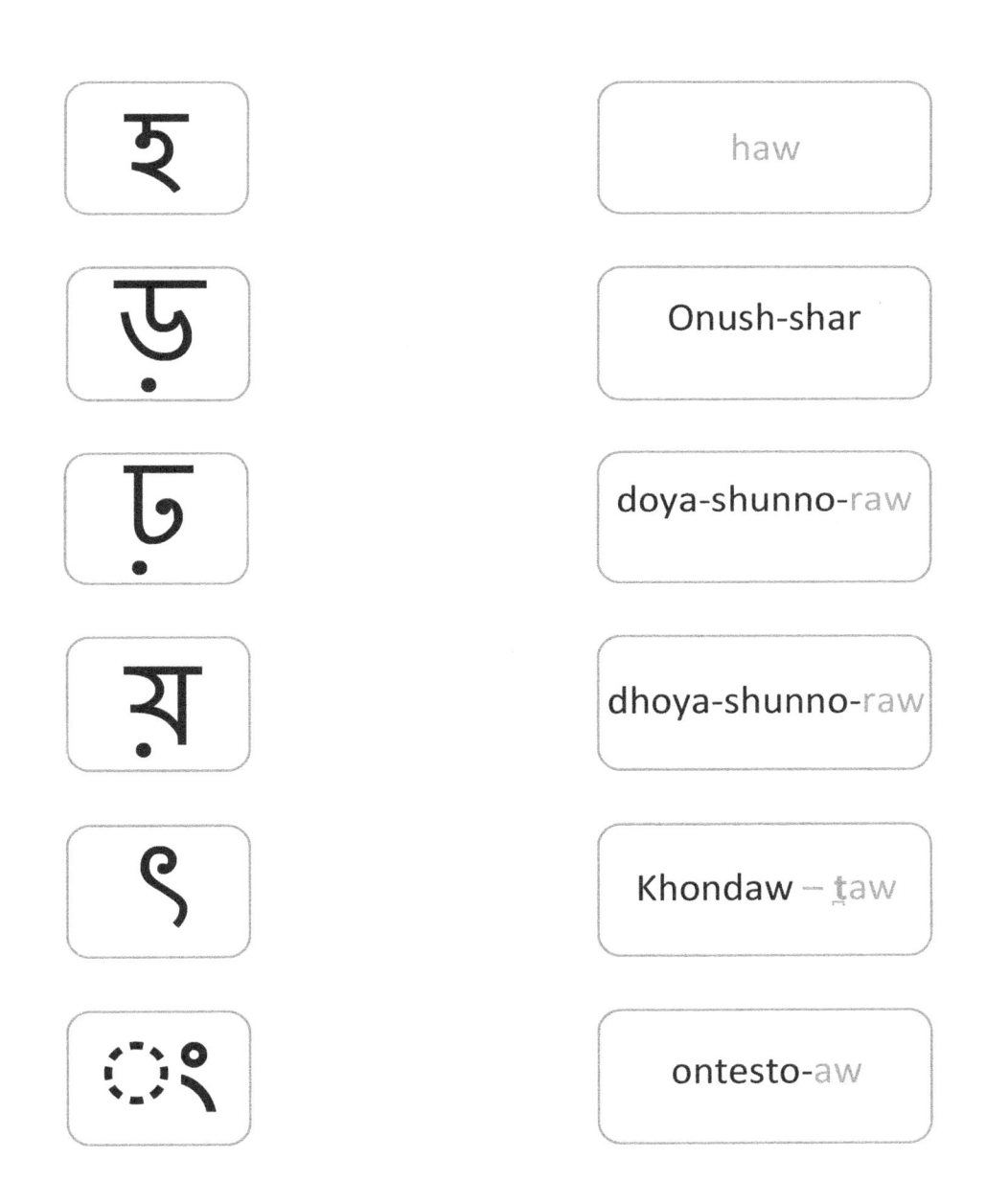

হ	haw
ড়	Onush-shar
ঢ়	doya-shunno-raw
য়	dhoya-shunno-raw
ৎ	Khondaw – taw
opendotted ং	ontesto-aw

59

Vowels marks

Vowel marks which are also known as kars, can only be used with a consonant. Each vowel mark makes the same sound as the corresponding vowel.

Vowel	Vowel mark (kar)
অ	
আ ah	◌া ah-kar
ই rosho-ee	ি◌ rosho-ee-kar
ঈ dirgo-ee	◌ী dirgo-ee-kar
উ rosho-oo	◌ু rosho-oo-kar
ঊ dirgo-oo	◌ূ dirgo-oo-kar
ঋ ri	◌ৃ ri-kar
এ eh	ে◌ eh-kar
ঐ oi	ৈ◌ oi-kar
ও au	ে◌া au-kar
ঔ ow	ে◌ৗ ow-kar

60

Vowel mark Ah-kar (◌া) with consonant ব (baw)

consonant	Consonant + vowel mark *ah-kar*	Sound it makes is highlighted
ব (baw)	ব + ◌া = বা (baw + ah-kar) = bah	b**u**nny

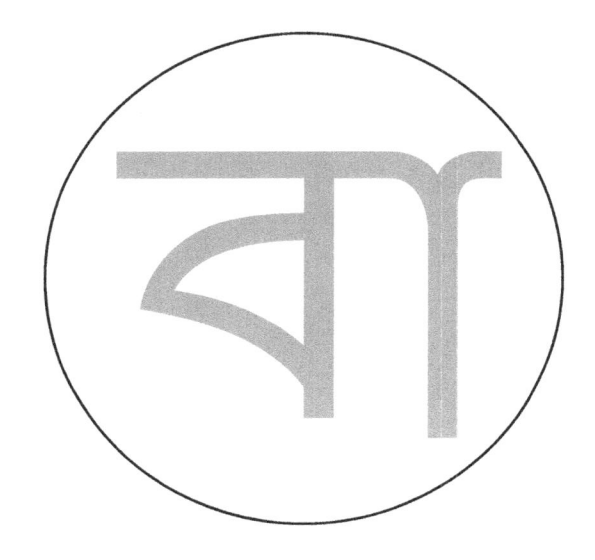

বা

Fill in the dotted line below to write the ah-kar

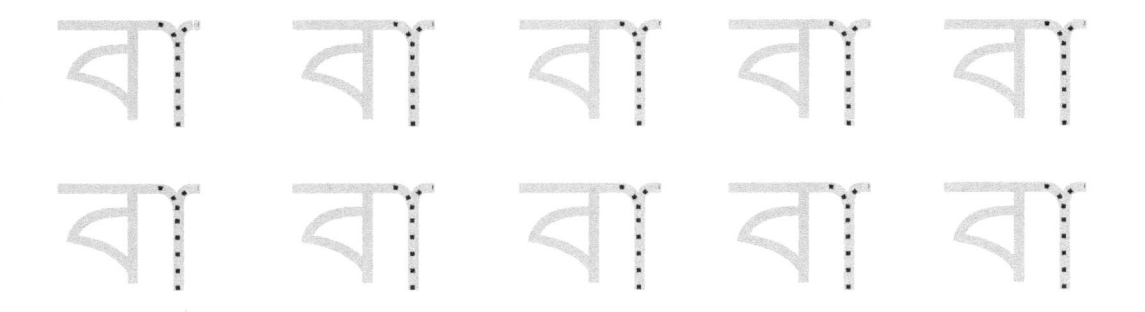

বা বা বা বা বা

বা বা বা বা বা

61

Vowel mark rosho-ee-kar (িঃ) with consonant ব (baw)

consonant	Consonant + vowel mark rosho-ee-kar	Sound it makes is highlighted
ব (baw)	ব + িঃ = বি (baw + rosho-ee-kar) = bi (short ee)	b**i**n

বি

Fill in the dotted line below to write the rosho ee-kar

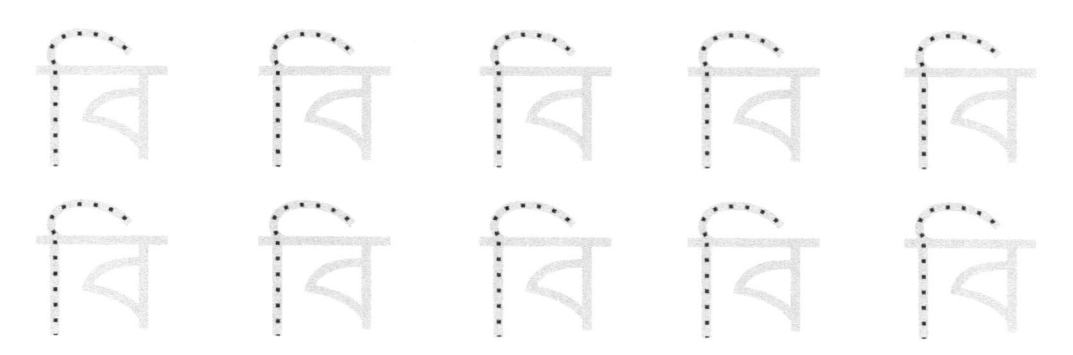

বি বি বি বি বি

বি বি বি বি বি

Vowel mark dirgo-ee-kar (ী) with consonant ব (baw)

consonant	Consonant + vowel mark dirgo-ee-kar	Sound it makes is highlighted
ব (baw)	ব + ী = বী (baw + dirgo-ee-kar) = bee (long ee)	be**a**m

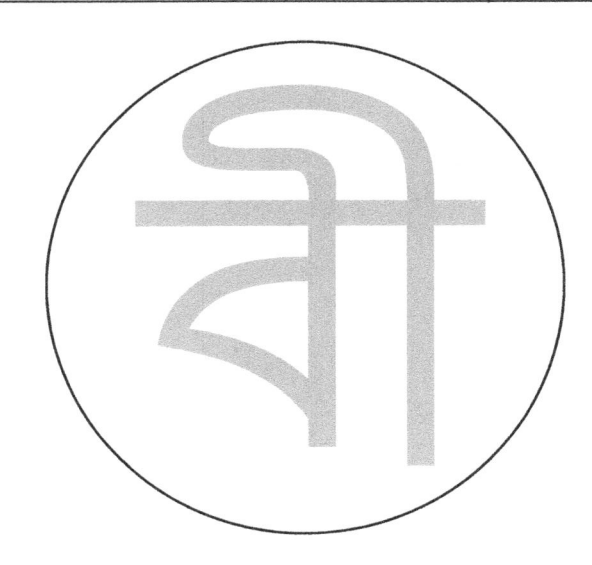

Fill in the dotted line below to write the dirgo ee-kar

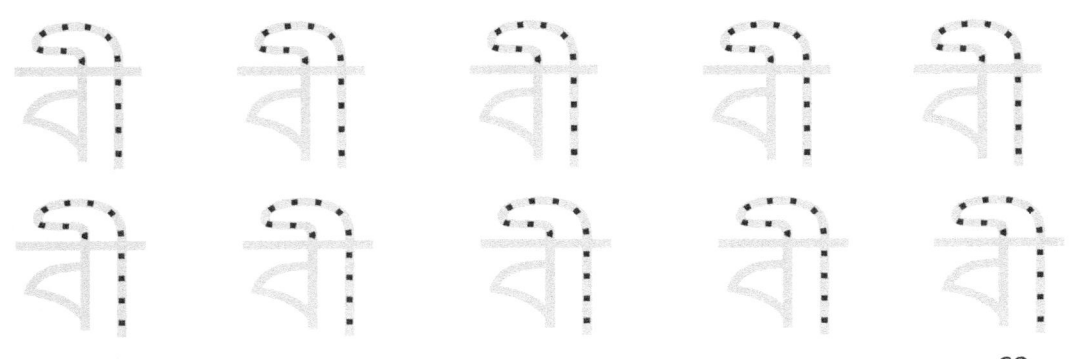

Vowel mark rosho-oo-kar (ু) with consonant ব (baw)

consonant	Consonant + vowel mark rosho-oo-kar	Sound it makes is highlighted
ব (baw)	ব + ু = বু (baw + rosho-oo-kar) = boo (short oo)	boo**k**

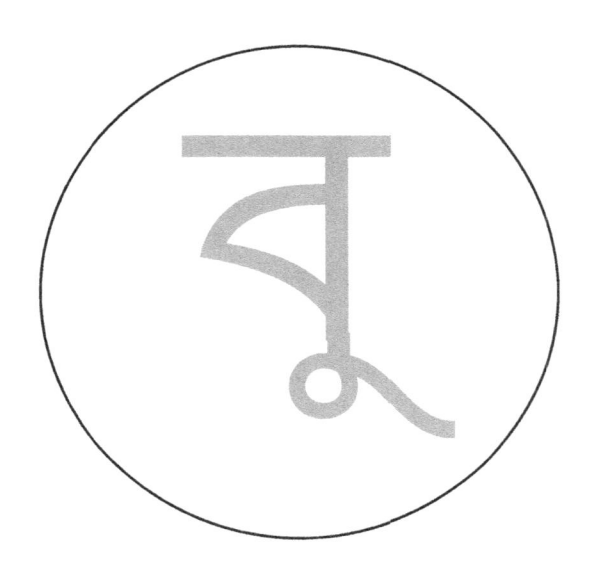

Fill in the dotted line below to write the rosho oo-kar

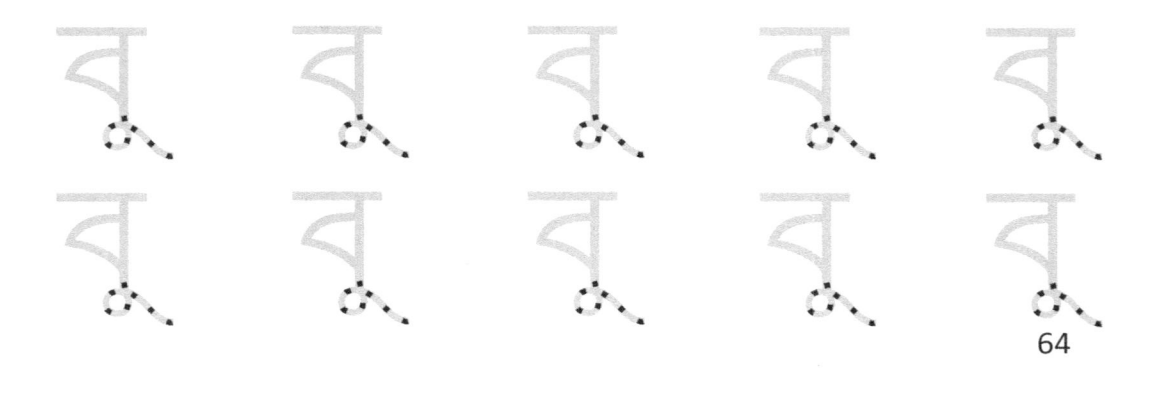

64

Vowel mark dirgo-oo-kar (্ূ) with consonant ব (baw)

consonant	Consonant + vowel mark dirgo-oo-kar	Sound it makes is highlighted
ব (baw)	ব + ্ূ = বূ (baw + dirgo-oo-kar) = boo (long oo)	b**oo**t

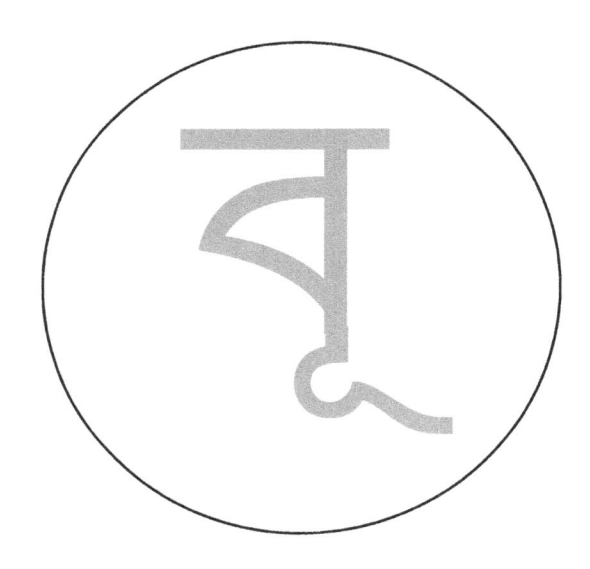

Fill in the dotted line below to write the dirgo-oo-kar

Draw a line to connect each vowel to its corresponding vowel mark (kar)

আ ah	ী
ই rosho-ee	ু
ঈ dirgo-ee	ি
উ rosho-oo	া
ঊ dirgo-oo	ূ

Vowel mark ri-kar (ৃ) with consonant ব (baw)

consonant	Consonant + vowel mark ri-kar	Sound it makes is highlighted
ব (baw)	ব + ৃ = বৃ (baw + ri-kar) = bri	bric**k**

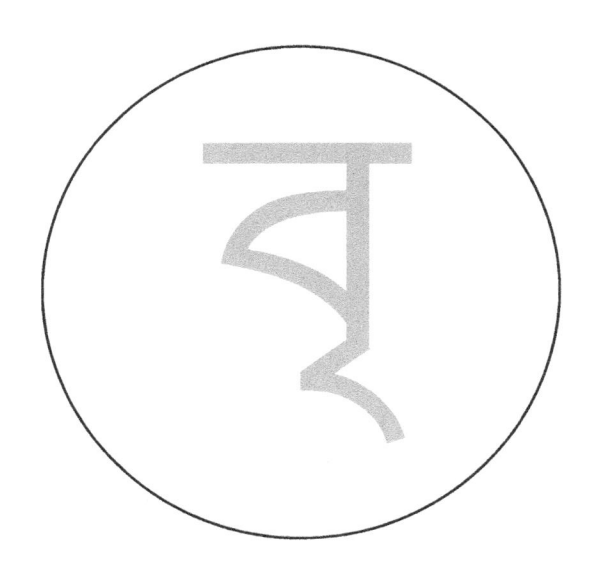

Fill in the dotted line below to write the ri-kar

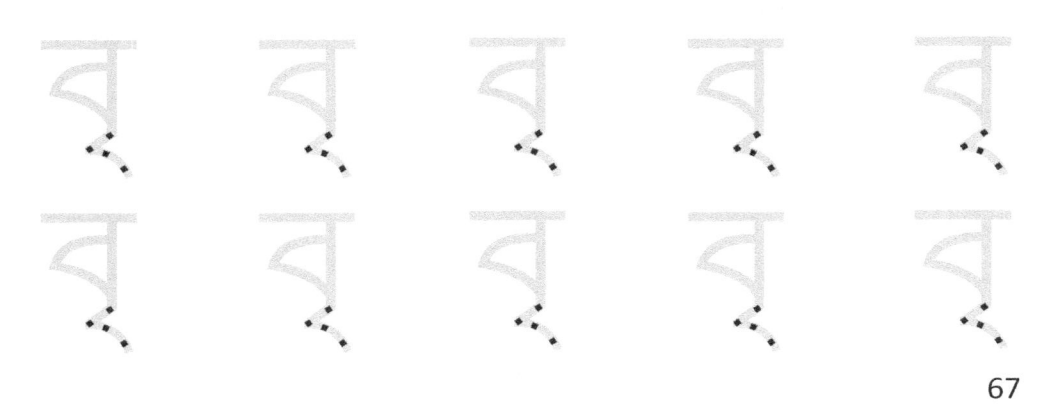

Vowel mark eh-kar (ো) with consonant ব (baw)

consonant	Consonant + vowel mark eh-kar	Sound it makes is highlighted
ব (baw)	ব + ো = বে (baw + eh-kar) = ba	ba**g**

বে

Fill in the dotted line below to write the eh-kar

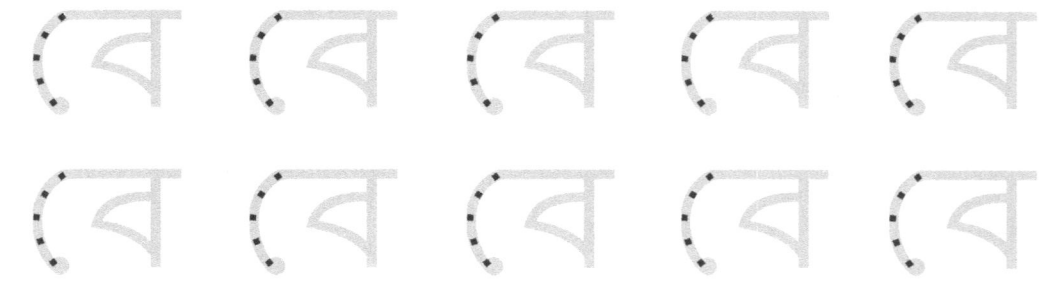

বে বে বে বে বে

বে বে বে বে বে

68

Vowel mark oi-kar (ৈ) with consonant ব (baw)

consonant	Consonant + vowel mark oi-kar	Sound it makes is highlighted
ব (baw)	ব + ৈ = বৈ (baw + oi-kar) = boy	boy

বৈ

Fill in the dotted line below to write the oi-kar

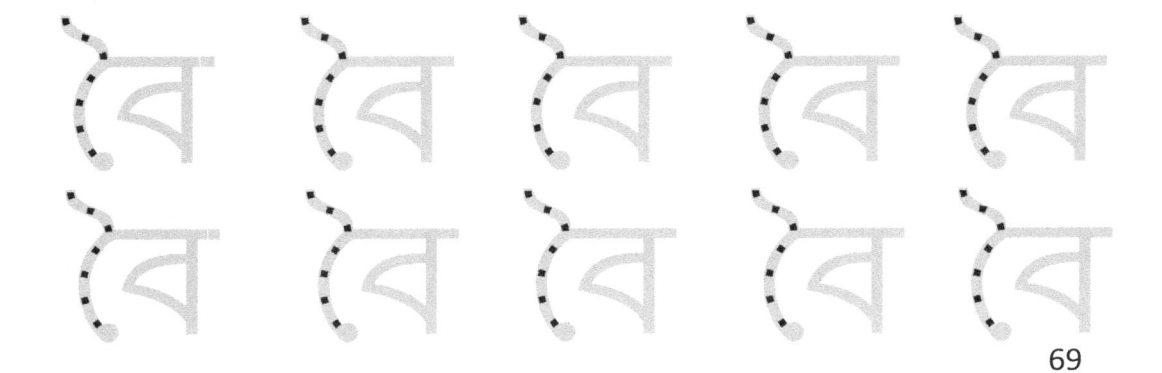

বৈ বৈ বৈ বৈ বৈ

বৈ বৈ বৈ বৈ বৈ

Vowel mark au-kar (ো) with consonant ব (baw)

consonant	Consonant + vowel mark au-kar	Sound it makes is highlighted
ব (baw)	ব + ো = বো (baw + au-kar) = bau	baw**l**

বো

Fill in the dotted line below to write the au-kar

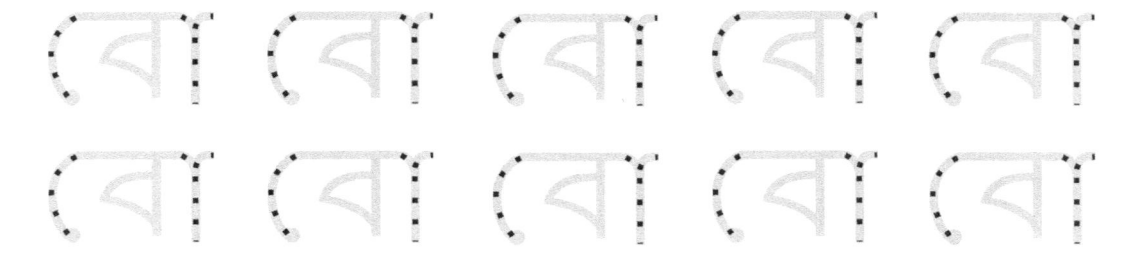

বো বো বো বো বো
বো বো বো বো বো

Vowel mark ow-kar (ো) with consonant ব (baw)

consonant	Consonant + vowel mark ow-kar	Sound it makes is highlighted
ব (baw)	ব + ো = বো (baw + ow-kar) = bow	bow

Fill in the dotted line below to write the ow-kar

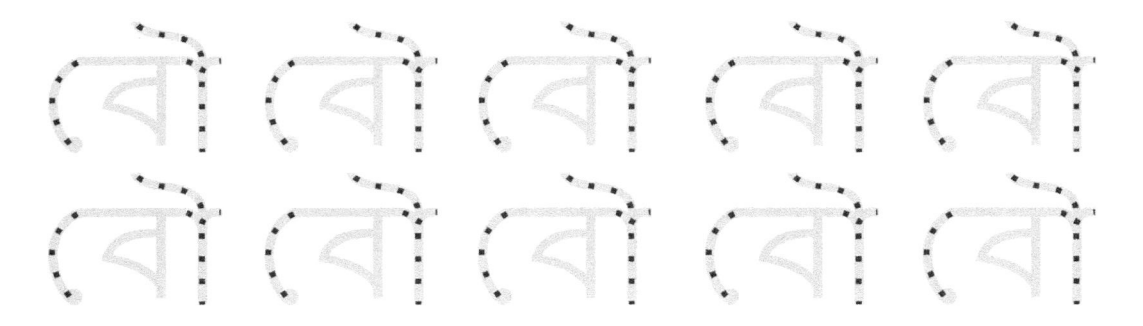

Draw a line to connect each vowel to its corresponding vowel mark (kar)

ঋ ri	ৈ
এ eh	ো
ঐ oi	ৃ
ও au	ৌ
ঔ ow	ে

Bengali alphabet modifiers

Modifiers are used to change the sound-values of the letters to which they are added. The modifiers given below are explained in the following pages.

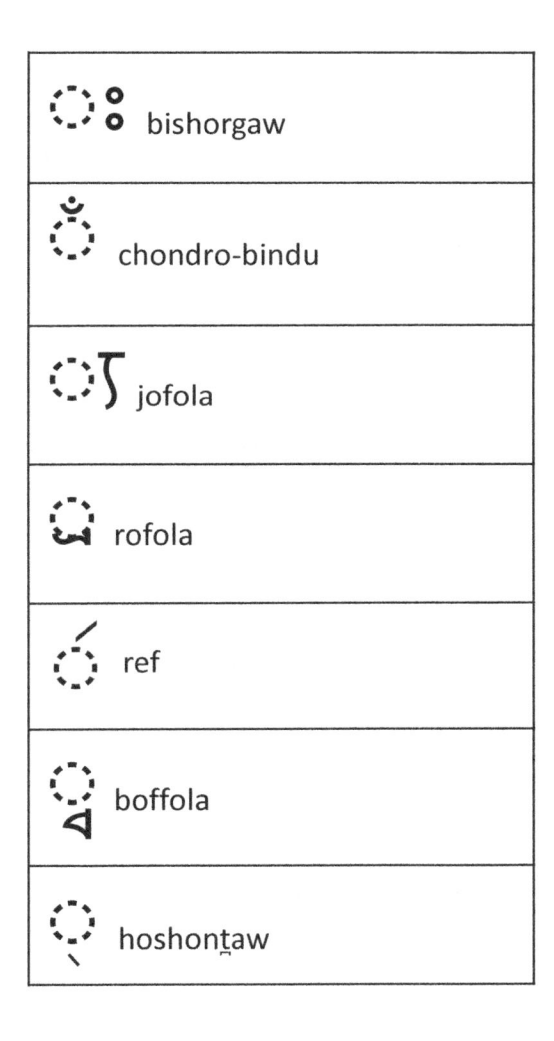

◌ঃ	bishorgaw
◌ঁ	chondro-bindu
◌্য	jofola
◌্র	rofola
◌ র্	ref
◌্ব	boffola
◌্	hoshontaw

◌ঃ bishorgaw	1> It doubles the sound of the consonant following it . In দুঃসাহস (dooঃshahosh) which means dare, স (sh) is repeated, as that letter follows the bishorgaw. In other words, an extra স (sh) is added. 2> It adds a h sound to the letter before it, such as in রেঃ (reঃ). Similar to an exclamation (!) mark.

Bishorgaw with the letter র (raw).

রঃ

Add the modifier Bishorgaw to each letter র below:

র র র র র

র র র র র

74

ঁ chondro-bindu	It nasalises the letter it goes above. তাঁরা (tãra) which means star.

Chondro-bindu with the letter ত (ṭaw)

Add the modifier chondro-bindu to each letter ত below:

75

| ি] | 1> If it is used with a syllable-initial consonant, it makes the a sound. Just as the a sound in the word black (ব্ল্যাক). |
| jofola | 2> If it is used with a syllable-final consonant, it doubles the consonant sound.

In মধ্য (mo<u>dd</u>ho) which means middle, ধ (<u>d</u>h) is repeated, as it is a syllable-final consonant. In other words, an extra ধ (<u>d</u>h) is added. |

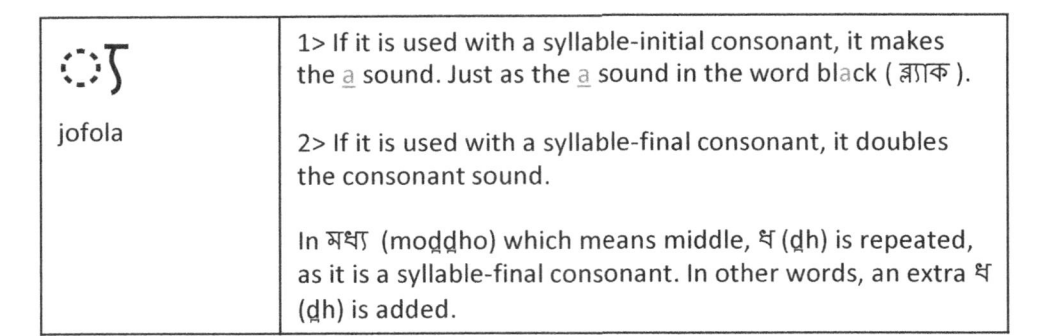

Jofola with the letter ধ (<u>d</u>haw).

ধ্য

Add the modifier jofola to each letter ধ below:

ধ   ধ   ধ   ধ   ধ

ধ   ধ   ধ   ধ   ধ

76

| ্র rofola | It is placed under a consonant. র (raw) sound is made after the sound of the consonant.
শ + ্র = শ্র (sh + ্র = shraw) |

Rofola with the letter শ (talibo-shaw).

Add the modifier rofola to each letter শ below:

শ শ শ শ শ

শ শ শ শ শ

◌́ ref	It is placed on top of the consonant. R sound precedes the consonant it is placed above. ব + ষা = ব + র্ + ষা = বর্ষা Baw + sha = baw + raw + sha = borsha

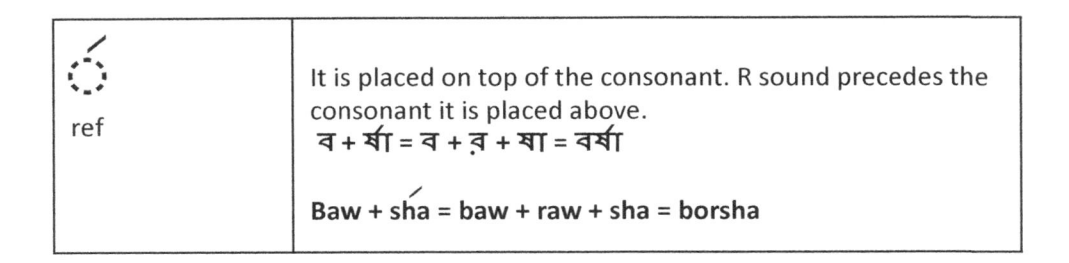

Ref with the letter স (moddheno-shaw).

স

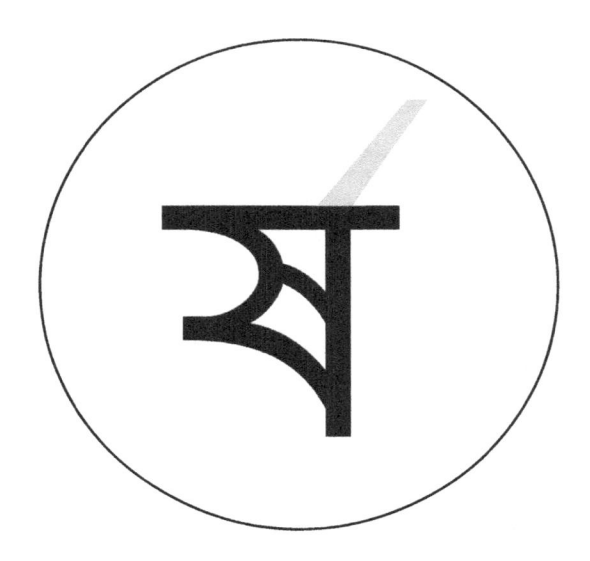

Add the modifier ref to each letter স below:

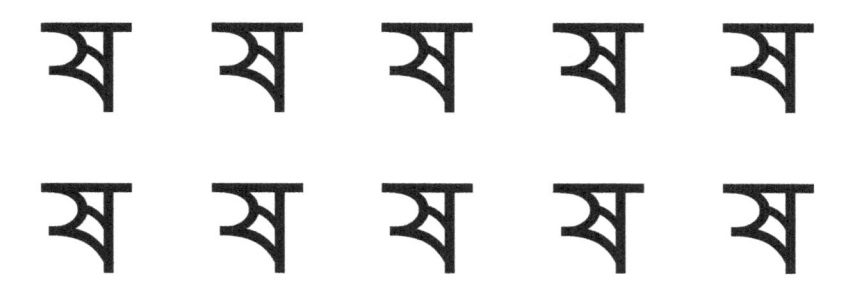

স স স স স

স স স স স

ব bofola	Letter ব (baw) is placed under a consonant. If the consonant it is placed under is a syllable-initial, than ব (baw) remains silent. However, if it is placed under a syllable-final consonant, than the sound of that consonant is doubled. বিদ্বান = বি+দ্ব+ন (bi+d+a+n) = biddan b

Bofola with the letter দ (daw).

Add the modifier bofola to each letter দ below:

দ   দ   দ   দ   দ

দ   দ   দ   দ   দ

়্ ় hoshontaw	Consonant letters are assumed to have an inherent vowel অ (aw) when there is no vowel mark present. For example, consonant ক (kaw) = k sound + vowel অ (aw) sound. The vowel অ (aw) sound here is the inherit vowel. When ়্ (hoshontaw) is added to a consonant letter, the inherent vowel অ (aw) sound is muted. For example, consonant ক (kaw) with hoshontaw would make only the k sound. **ক্ = k sound**

Hoshontaw with the letter ক (kaw).

ক্

Add the modifier hoshontaw to each letter ক below:

ক ক ক ক ক
ক ক ক ক ক

Draw a line to connect each letter to it's name

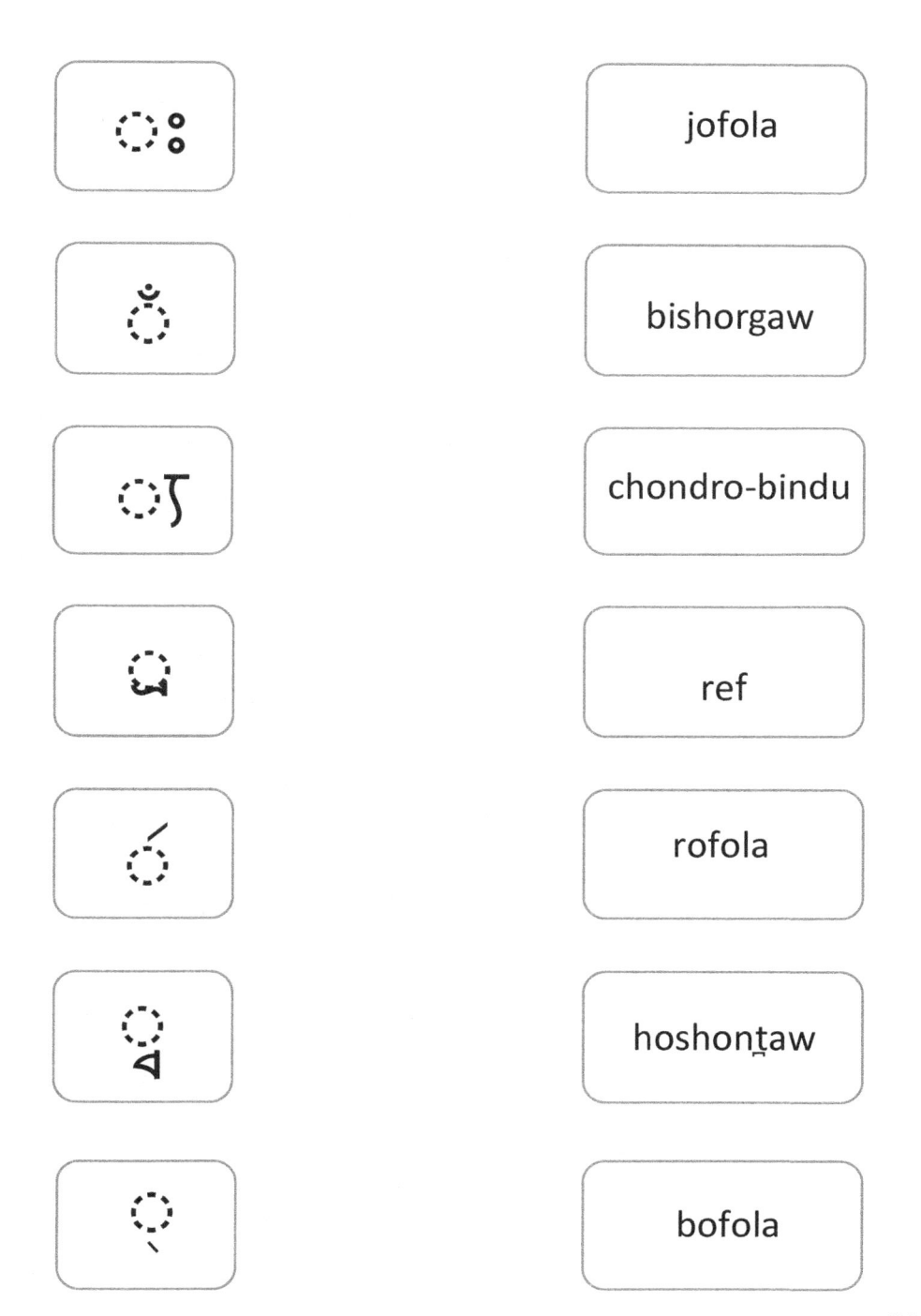

়ঃ	jofola
ঁ	bishorgaw
ীা	chondro-bindu
র্	ref
ৗ	rofola
্য	hoshontaw
্র	bofola

Joint letters

In Bengali alphabet letters can be joined together to form a joint sound. A few joint letters are given bellow.

ক + ক = ক্ক	(kaw + kaw = kkaw)
ক + ট = ক্ট	(kaw + taw = ktaw)
ক + ম = ক্ম	(kaw + maw = kmaw)
ক + ল = ক্ল	(kaw + law = klaw)
গ + ল = গ্ল	(gaw + law = glaw)
চ + চ = চ্চ	(chaw + chaw = chchaw)
প + প = প্প	(paw + paw = ppaw)
ল + ড = ল্ড	(law + daw = ldaw)
ব + ব = ব্ব	(baw + baw = bbaw)
ব + ল = ব্ল	(baw + law = blaw)

Joint letter | **Sound the joint letter makes is highlighted** | **Follow the arrow To write the letter**

ক+ক
kaw + kaw

↓

ক্ক
kkaw

A**k**kel
আক্কেল
(wisdom)

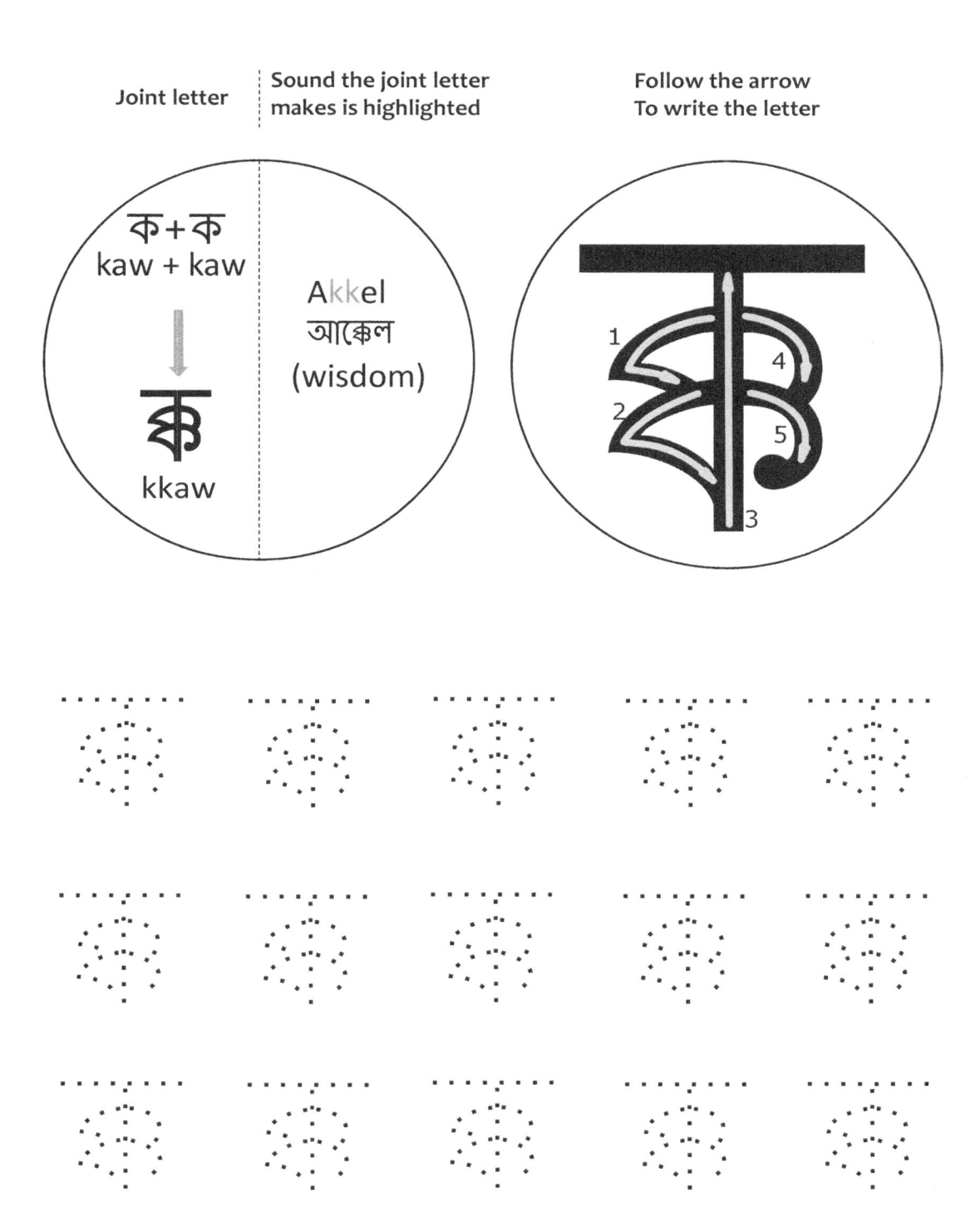

83

Joint letter | **Sound the joint letter makes is highlighted** | **Follow the arrow To write the letter**

ক + ট
kaw + taw

↓

ক্ট
ktaw

do**ct**or
ড**ক্ট**র

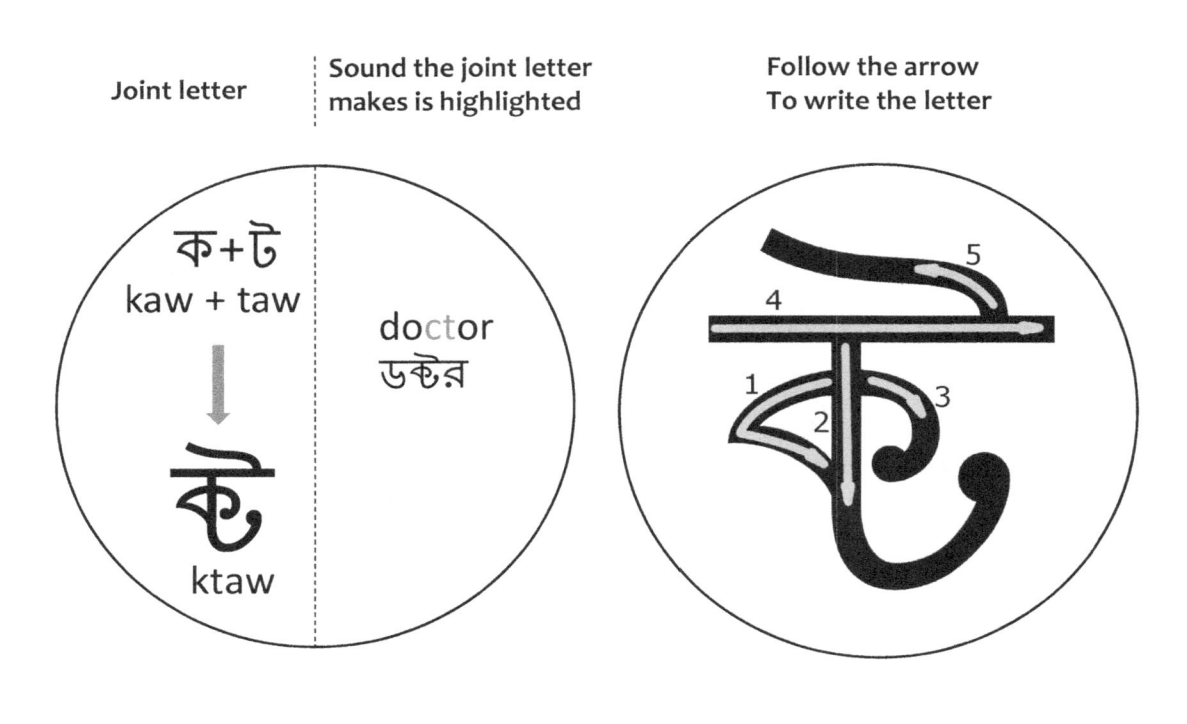

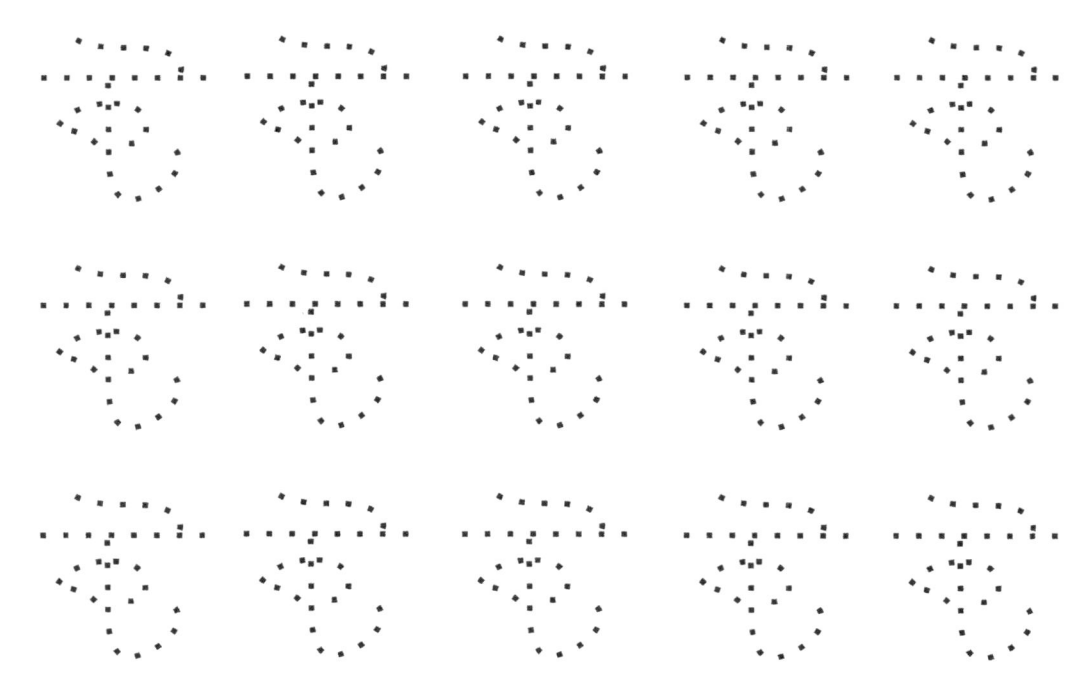

84

Joint letter	Sound the joint letter makes is highlighted	Follow the arrow To write the letter

ক + ম
kaw + maw

↓

ক্ম
kmaw

ru**km**ini
রুক্মিণী
(female name)

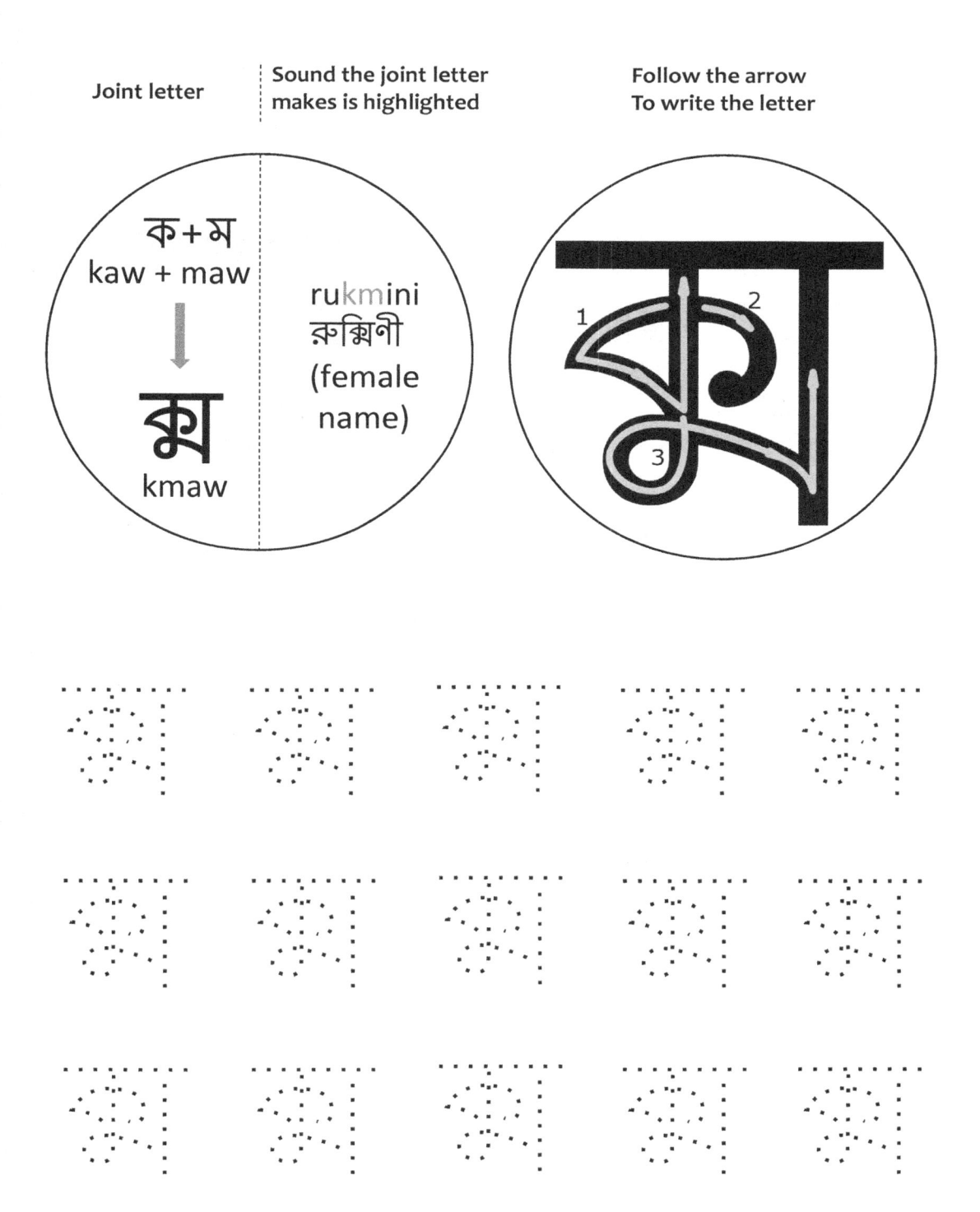

85

| Joint letter | Sound the joint letter makes is highlighted | Follow the arrow To write the letter |

ক + ল
kaw + law
↓
ক্ল
klaw

klanti
ক্লান্তি
(fatigue)

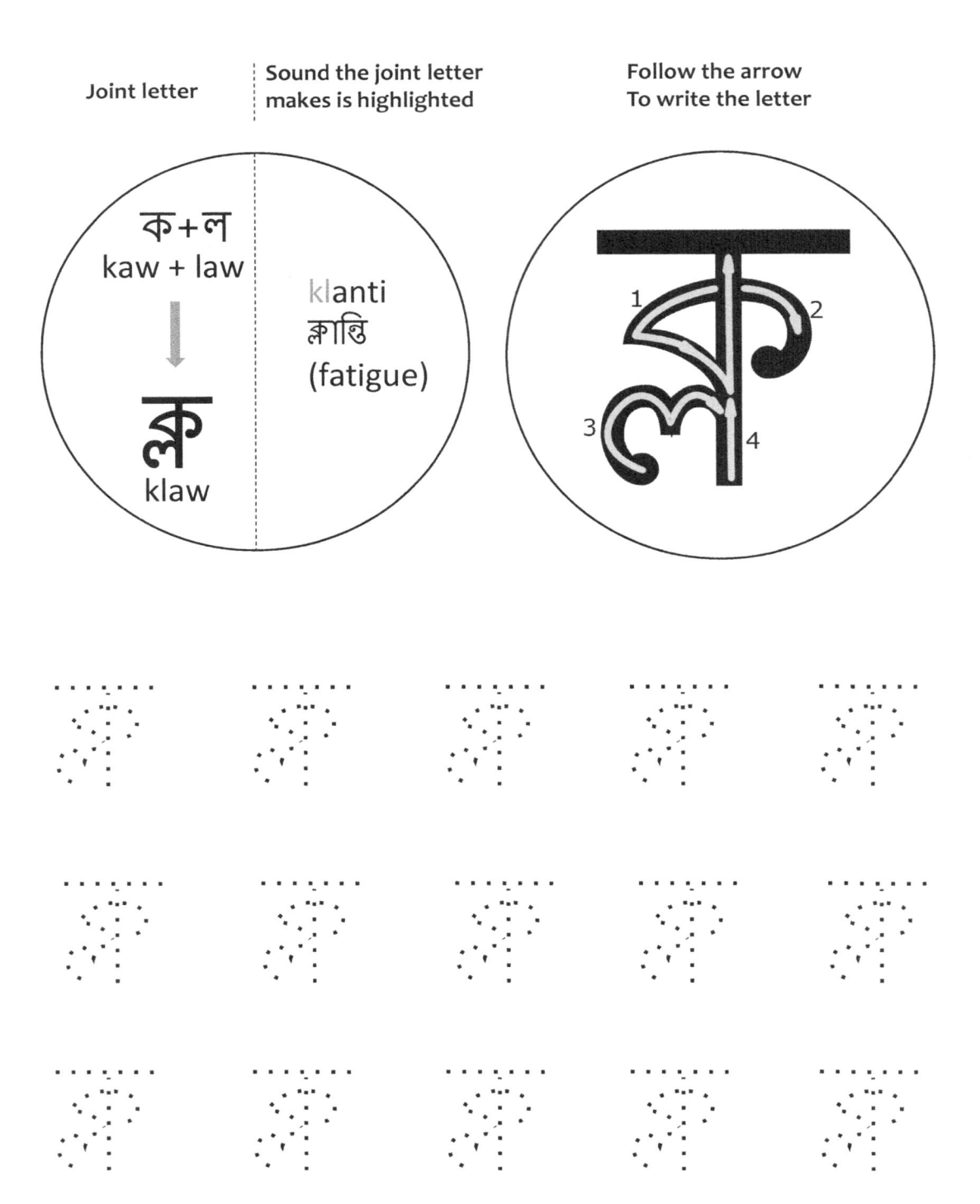

86

Joint letter	Sound the joint letter makes is highlighted	Follow the arrow To write the letter
গ + ল gaw + law ↓ গ্ল glaw	glani গ্লানি (dirt)	

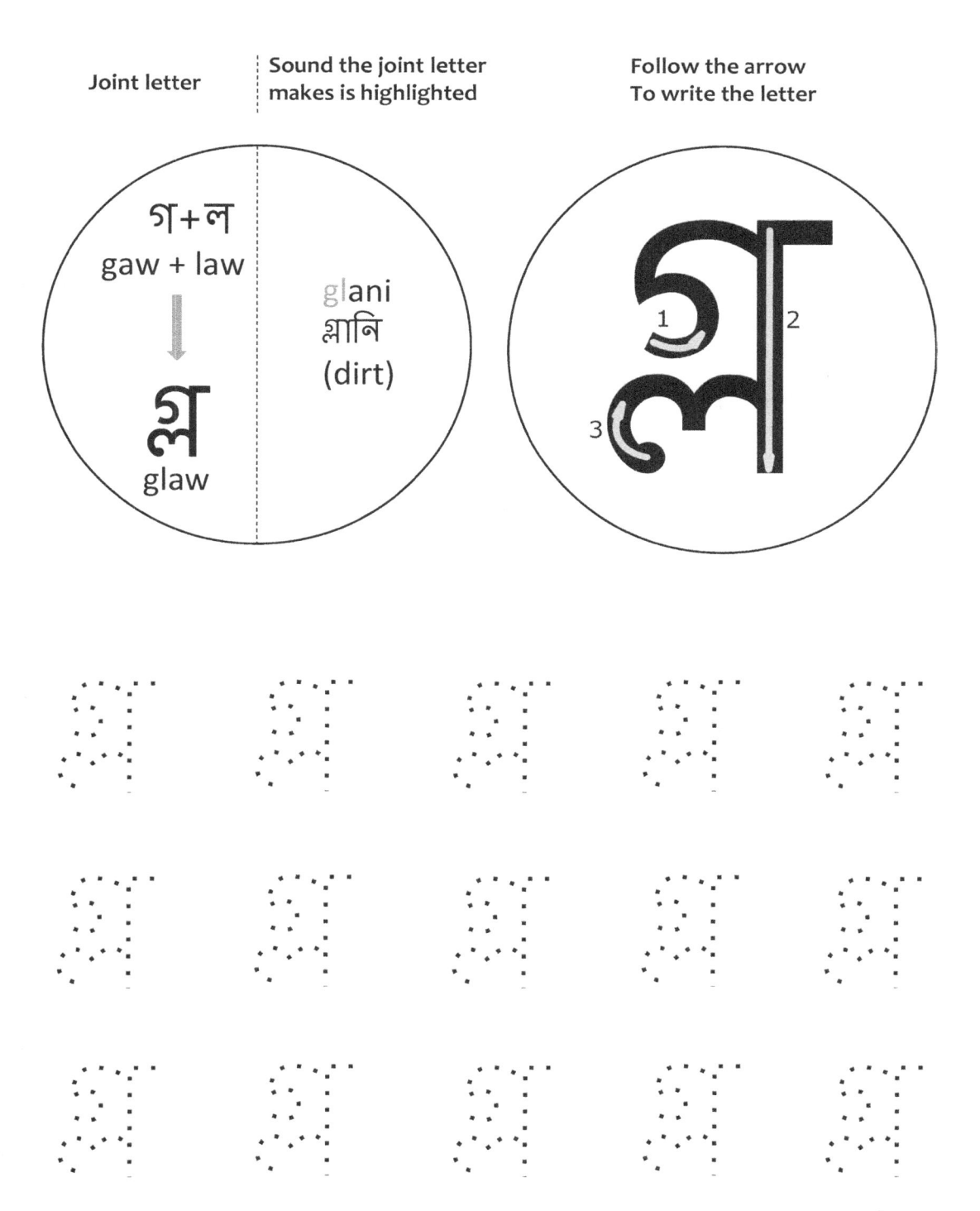

87

Draw lines to connect the letters on the left to the joint sound they make on the right

ক + ক kaw + kaw	ক্ম
ক + ট kaw + taw	ক্ল
ক + ম kaw + maw	ক্ক
ক + ল kaw + law	ক্ট
গ + ল gaw + law	গ্ল

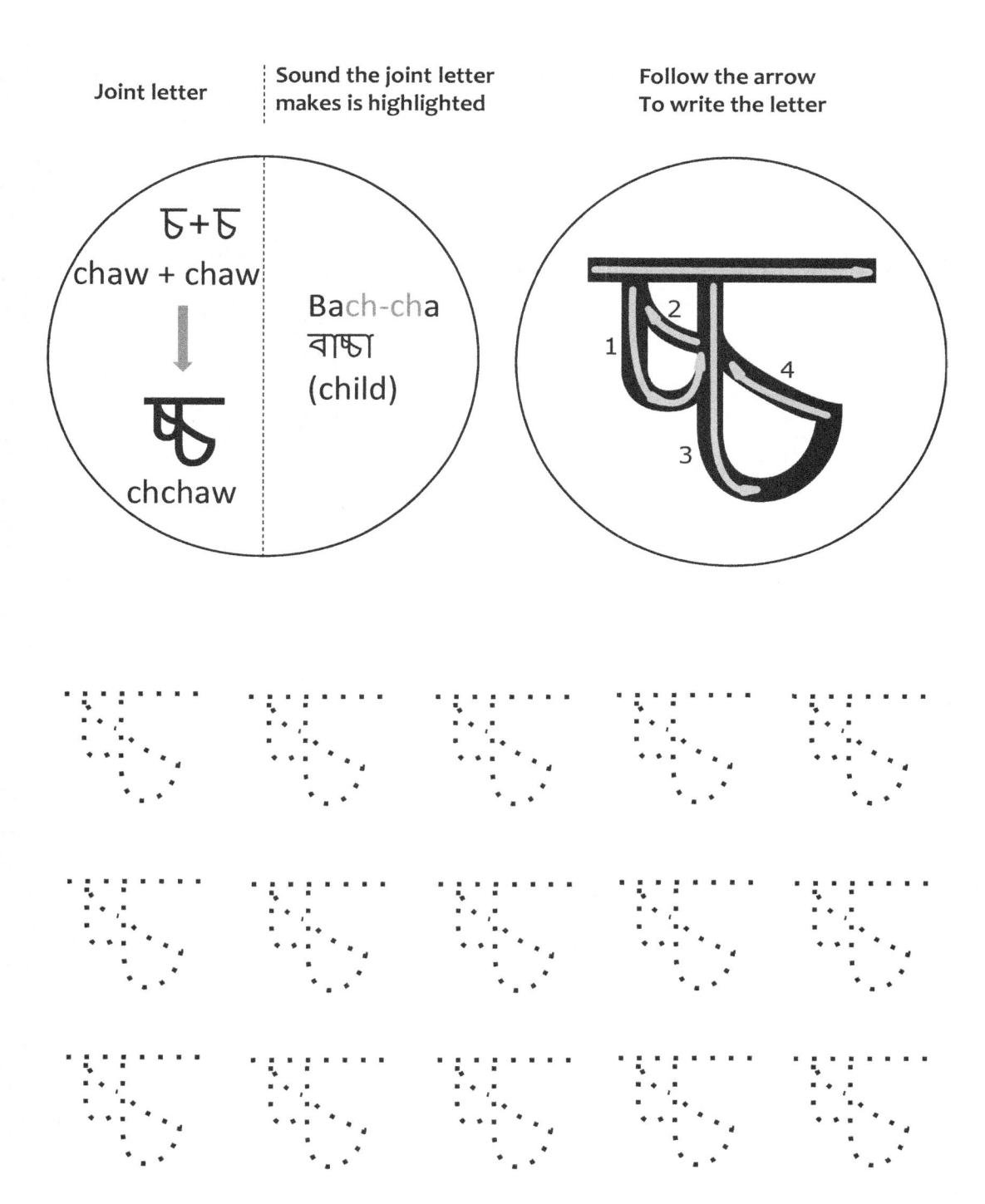

Joint letter | Sound the joint letter makes is highlighted | Follow the arrow To write the letter

ট + ট
chaw + chaw
↓
ছ
chchaw

Ba**ch-ch**a
বাচ্চা
(child)

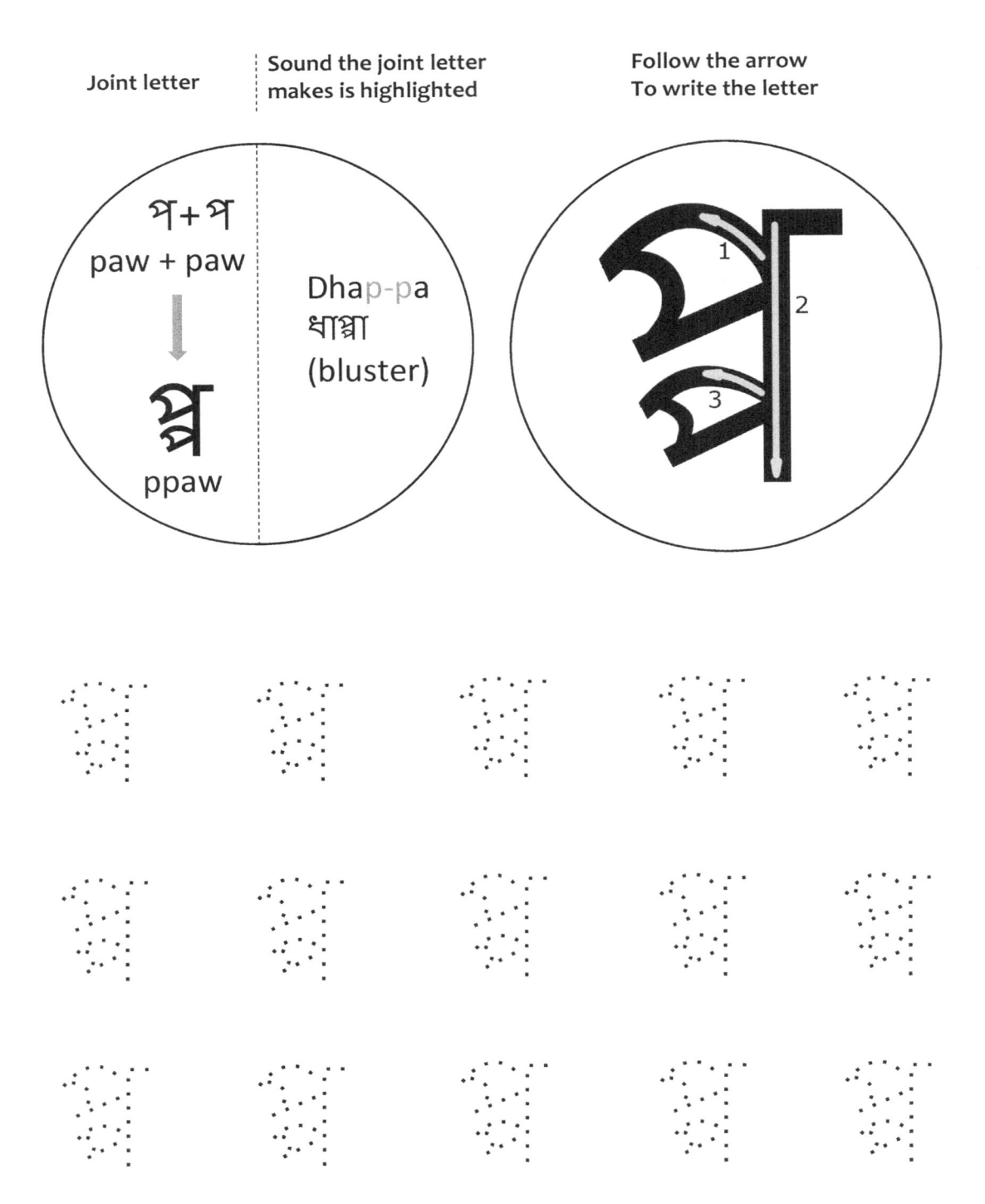

Joint letter	Sound the joint letter makes is highlighted	Follow the arrow To write the letter

প + প
paw + paw
↓
প্প
ppaw

Dhap-pa
ধাপ্পা
(bluster)

90

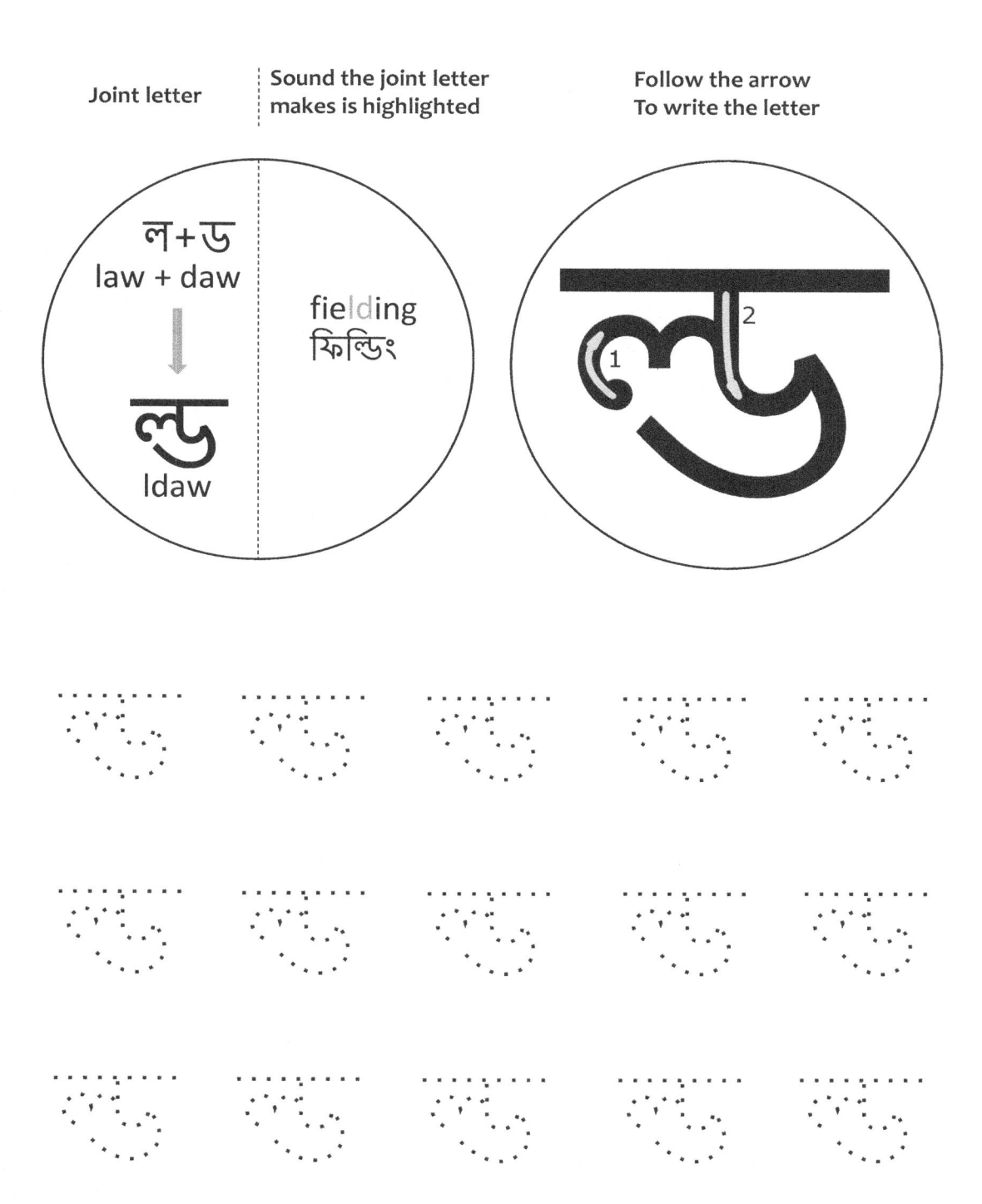

Joint letter | **Sound the joint letter makes is highlighted** | **Follow the arrow To write the letter**

ল + ড
law + daw

⬇

ল্ড
ldaw

fielding
ফিল্ডিং

91

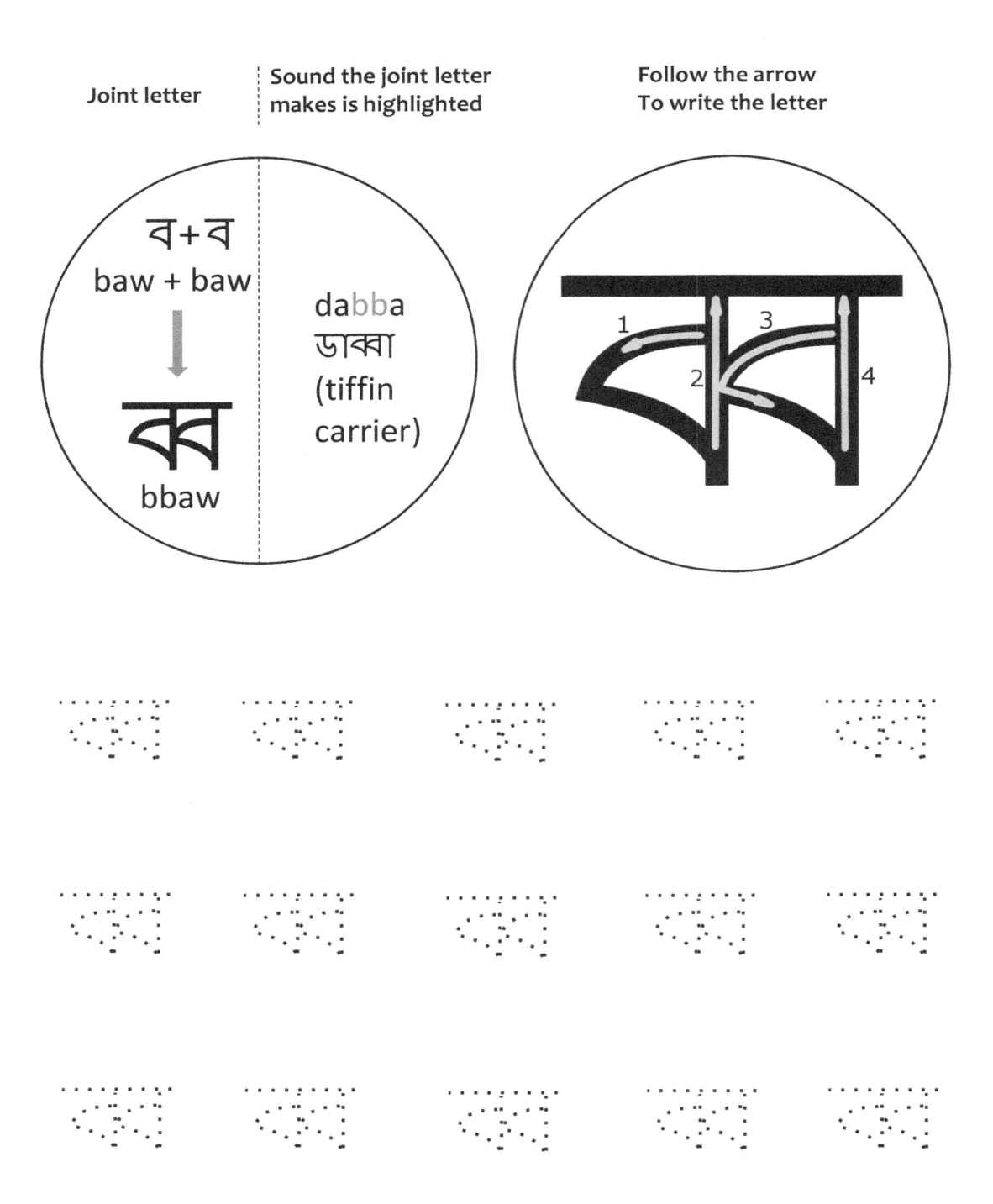

Joint letter	Sound the joint letter makes is highlighted	Follow the arrow To write the letter

ব + ব
baw + baw
↓
ব্ব
bbaw

da**bb**a
ডা**ব্ব**া
(tiffin carrier)

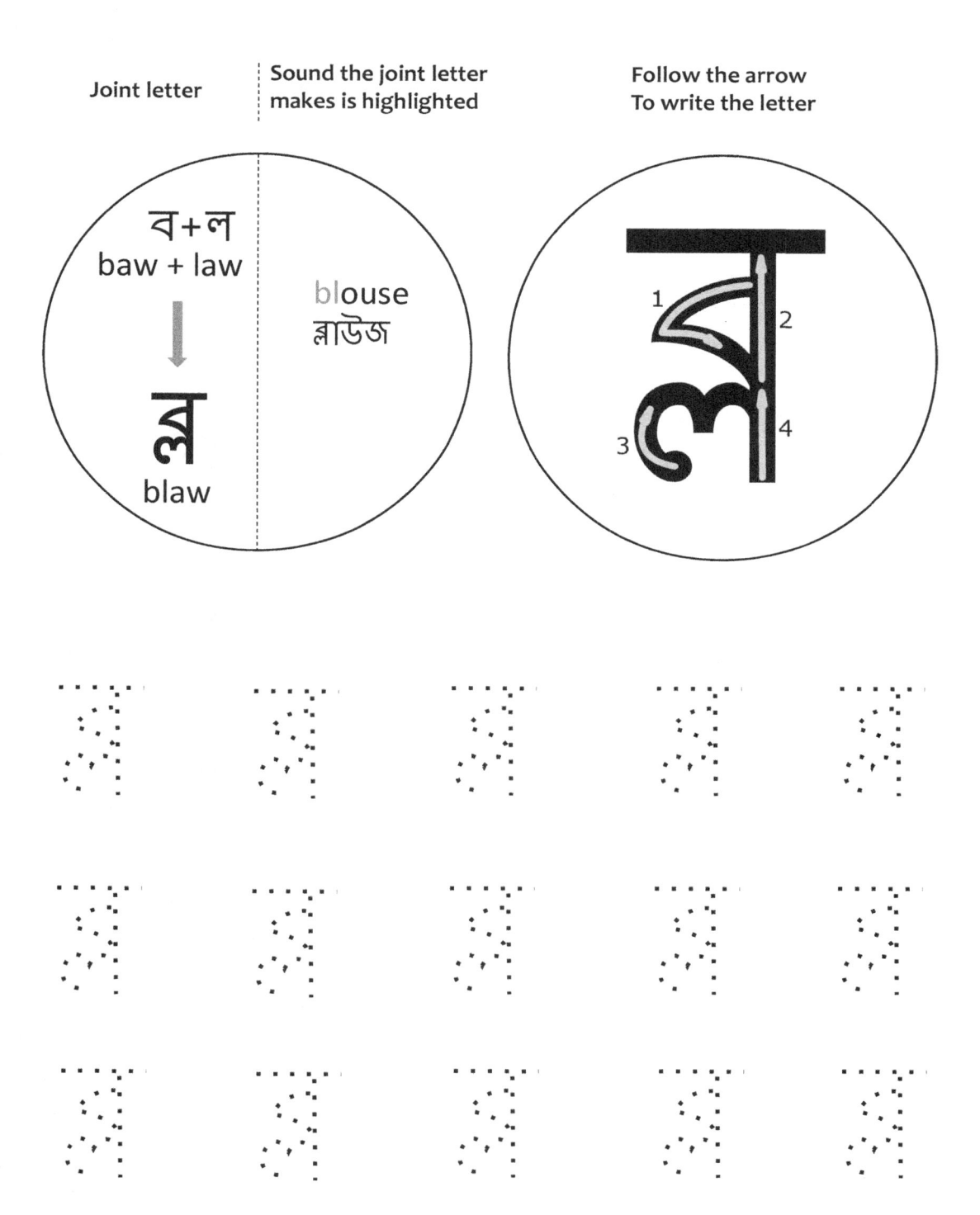

Joint letter	Sound the joint letter makes is highlighted	Follow the arrow To write the letter

ব + ল
baw + law
↓
ব্ল
blaw

blouse
ব্লাউজ

Draw lines to connect the letters on the left to the joint sound they make on the right

চ + চ chaw + chaw	প্র
প + প paw + paw	ল্ড
ল + ড law + daw	চ্চ
ব + ব baw + baw	ব্ল
ব + ল baw + law	ব্ব

Vowels

অ   আ   ই   ঈ   উ   ঊ

ঋ   এ   ঐ   ও   ঔ

Consonants

ক   খ   গ   ঘ   ঙ
চ   ছ   জ   ঝ   ঞ
ট   ঠ   ড   ঢ   ণ
ত   থ   দ   ধ   ন
প   ফ   ব   ভ   ম
য   র   ল   শ   ষ
স   হ   ড়   ঢ়   য়
ৎ   ঃং

Vowels marks (kars)

ാ   ি   ী   ু   ૂ

ৃ   ে   ৈ   ো   ৌ

Bengali alphabet modifiers

ঃ   ঁ   ং   ় ্

ৢ   ৗ

If you found this book helpful, please leave a review.

To submit a review:

- Go to the product detail page for this book on www.amazon.com

- Click Write a customer review in the Customer Reviews section.

Made in the USA
Las Vegas, NV
20 September 2024

95517781R00057